THE FIRST EPISTLE OF PAUL TO THE CORINTHIANS

An Exposition

D0973147

THE FIRST EPISTLE
OF PAUL
TO
THE CORINTHIANS

An Exposition

by
CHARLES R. ERDMAN

PREFACE BY EARL F. ZEIGLER

THE WESTMINSTER PRESS

PHILADELPHIA

Published by The Westminster Press ®
Philadelphia, Pennsylvania
PRINTED IN THE UNITED STATES OF AMERICA

To
my faithful friends and parishioners
of the
First Presbyterian Church
Princeton

PREFACE

Not many decades ago in the U.S.A. the great cities were the stronghold of numerous and prosperous churches. Now the inner city has become the "problem child" of ecclesiastical administrators. But the inner city needs the churches desperately, and the churches have an appointment with God to keep the gospel where the people are.

The First Letter of Paul to the Corinthians was written to the Christians of a great city. Corinth was famous for almost every asset and liability to which seaport towns are heir. It had wealth, culture, and a cosmopolitan population of a half million, 50 percent of whom were slaves. (The expositor of this volume elaborates on other assets and liabilities.) There was a considerable sprinkling of Jews, and at least one synagogue. Until Paul came to Corinth no Christian is believed to have been living there. Perhaps the first converts were Aquila and Priscilla, Jewish tentmakers with whom Paul stayed. Before Paul had completed eighteen persevering months in the city a church of no mean size had been organized to continue evangelizing the unreached, and growing itself in spiritual depth. Sometime after Paul had left to work elsewhere, the young church broke out with a rash of problems. When word reached the apostle he secured a secretary, and at high speed, but with marvelous wisdom and with repetition of the gospel fundamentals that he had taught when with them, he helped these inexperienced people to resolve their difficulties and settle down to the main reason for being a church.

While composing this letter, the apostle outdid himself, humanly speaking. In writing to the church members about their use of spiritual gifts (and some of them were making a fetish of these), Paul dictated to his secretary: "But earnestly desire the higher gifts. And I will show you a still more excellent way." And what Paul wrote in the next sentences was the immortal hymn of love, I Cor., ch. 13, as it is known wherever the gospel has been proclaimed. When the apostle grappled with the Corinthian church problem about the resurrection of the body, his answer flowed forth in words that inspired hope then, and have comforted millions through the centuries wherever people gather to lay their dead away.

This is the letter of Paul, the text of which is complete in this volume. The writer of the exposition is Dr. Charles R. Erdman, who is also the writer of the other sixteen volumes in this series of New Testament commentaries. For thirty years, Dr. Erdman was professor of practical theology at Princeton Seminary. Previously he had been pastor of two thriving churches in Philadelphia; and during a portion of his Princeton professorship he served as pastor of First Presbyterian Church in Princeton. He was also Moderator of the Presbyterian Church in the U.S.A. These combined experiences, and many others, fitted Dr. Erdman to write a most useful, practical, and popular series. The volumes have been printed so often that the type and plates are practically worn out. In view of the continuing demand, this paperback edition has been issued on completely new type and plates. In this way Dr. Erdman will continue to teach new generations who now "know in part" but are seeking to understand more fully.

EARL F. ZEIGLER

FOREWORD

The church of Christ is the most significant and important society established among men. Not all persons place upon it such an appraisal, nor has the conduct of its members always vindicated its claim to a divine origin and a unique mission. However, those who adore its Founder as their Lord, and believe that through the church he is accomplishing his gracious purpose for the redemption of the world, will read the following letter with ever-deepening interest. It was written by the apostle Paul to the Christians of Corinth and it concerns questions of vital importance relative to the life and ministry and message of the church.

While the circumstances under which these questions arose were largely local and temporary, their treatment by the apostle is of immediate interest and of abiding value for the reason that he discusses each one in the light of some permanent principle. All who are concerned for the peace and purity and progress of the church should seek to apply these principles to the pressing problems of the present day.

INTRODUCTION

The city of Corinth is being brought back from the grave. At least it is true that recent excavations are making this old Greek city live again in the vision, the thought, and the imagination of the world. To stand in its great theater or to read the inscription on the "Synagogue of the Jews," to tread the mosaic floors of its imperial villas, and to visit the forum where Gallio sat on his judgment seat is to bridge the intervening centuries and to dwell amid the scenes of a long-buried past.

In another sense, however, Corinth never has been buried. Two short letters written by the apostle Paul to a group of Christians in that city have made the place, through all the passing generations, familiar to countless readers in whose memories the city has never ceased to live. However, in the light of recent discoveries at Corinth, the epistles of Paul have become more vivid, more vital, more credible, and more real than they have been for centuries.

In the time of the apostle, Corinth was the most important city of Greece. Athens was a greater center of culture and more conspicuous in the memories of a gloriout past; but Corinth was the capital of the Roman province of Achaia, and surpassed all other cities in political and commercial importance. Destroyed by the Roman Mummius in 146 B.C., it had been rebuilt a century later at the command of Julius Caesar and soon had regained and even surpassed its former position of wealth and beauty and splendor and power.

Its rapid growth was due in large measure to its location. It was situated on the narrow isthmus which connected the Peloponnesus with the Greek mainland and separated the Ionian from the Aegean Sea. To the west was the port of Lechaeum; to the east, Cenchreae. Because of this situation it was called "the City of the Two Seas." Thus located it was on the main route of travel between the East and the West and became the chief emporium of trade between Asia and Rome.

The wealth of the city was enormous and its population was probably fourth in size among the cities of the Roman Empire. This population consisted originally of colonists, most of whom were Roman freedmen. In addition to their descendants, there had come to the city a great infusion of native Greeks.

Furthermore, Corinth had attracted a great crowd of foreigners from East and West. These had thronged the city and had adopted the Greek language and customs. As in most cities, there was a large colony of Jews who retained their distinctive beliefs and worship. Fully one half of the population consisted of slaves.

While Corinth was a commercial city, it nevertheless prided itself upon its culture, and abounded in studios and workshops, in halls of rhetoric and schools of philosophy. However, the city was no more widely known for its wealth and culture than for its wickedness and moral corruption. It was the seat of a debased form of the worship of Venus, and of impure cults from Egypt and Asia. "To live as a Corinthian" meant to the men of Paul's day to live in luxury and licentiousness, and the phrases "Corinthian banquet" and "Corinthian drinkers" were similarly proverbial.

The founding of a Christian church in such a community was a notable proof of the power of the gospel and was one of the most signal triumphs of Paul's career. It was a triumph snatched out of threatened defeat. The apostle had reached the city dispirited, disheartened, and alone. He was on his second great missionary journey. Starting from Antioch he had traveled westward to Troas. In response to a divine call, he had crossed the sea to Europe and established churches in Philippi and Thessalonica, and passed southward to Greece. His reception at

Athens had been cold and discouraging. He turned to Corinth and arrived as an unknown stranger without companions, without money, without friends, and with a heart weighed down by the sight of universal godlessness, impurity, and vice. He began his preaching in weakness and fear, and much trembling, but with a determination to be true to the message of Christ and his cross.

He soon formed a friendship with two Jews, Aquila and Prisca, who had recently been driven from Rome and who had established themselves in Corinth as makers of tents. As Paul was of the same race and trade, he was welcomed to their home and found them receptive to his teachings concerning Christ. Shortly afterward he was encouraged further by the arrival of his friends, Silas and Timothy, and he began to proclaim the gospel with unusual power and effect. His first audiences were those of the synagogue, but because of the exasperation and bitter opposition of his Jewish adversaries he left this place of meeting and established a Christian assembly in the neighboring house of Titus Justus. This Jewish proselyte, whose name indicates that he was a Roman citizen, was able to afford Paul an honorable refuge and to give encouragement to the growing group of believers. Among the converts who gathered in this house were Crispus, the ruler of the synagogue, his family, and certain other persons of importance. The great body of the converts, however, came from the humbler classes, even from among the freedmen and slaves. Some were Jews, but most of them were Gentiles; not many trained in the schools, not many of official dignity and power, not many of aristocratic birth were found in this new society. There were among them contrasts of wealth and poverty, of high rank and lowly position, but the weak and baseborn formed the majority of this Christian assembly, and among them were many who had been rescued from the lowest depths of pagan vice.

At this time the heart of the apostle was greatly strengthened by a night vision of his Lord, who bade Paul to speak fearlessly and assured him of safety and success in his work.   Accordingly, Paul remained for eighteen months preaching chiefly to Gentiles and establishing an ever-enlarging community of Christians.   Moved by envy and enmity, the Jews raised an insurrection and dragged the apostle before the judgment seat of the proconsul, Gallio.   This noble Roman, a brother of the philosopher Seneca, disdainfully refused to entertain the charges of religious heresy which the Jews attempted to present against Paul.   He drove the Jews from the judgment seat, and allowed the Greeks to beat Sosthenes, the ruler of the synagogue, an act which he seemed to regard as a piece of rough justice and a sign of the popular approval of his position.   The attitude of Gallio has been interpreted frequently as indicating his religious indifference.   More properly it should be regarded as an example of religious tolerance and as a practical declaration that Paul had the sanction of the Roman Government to proclaim the gospel in Greece.   Thus when some time later Paul ended his labors in Corinth and sailed for Jerusalem and Antioch, he left behind him a strong and flourishing church, practically under the protection of Rome and able to proceed with the evangelization of the entire province of Achaia.

On Paul's third missionary journey, during his long stay of three years in the city of Ephesus, he maintained constant intercourse with the infant church in Corinth westward across the Aegean Sea.   Letters were exchanged between the apostle and his Corinthian converts.   There are indications that Paul paid a brief visit to the city, returning again to Ephesus.   Early in his stay he seems to have received a favorable report of the condition of the church from Titus, whom he had sent to acquaint the Corinthians with his plan for the relief of the poor Christians in Jerusalem and to secure their sympathy and aid.   Subsequently the eloquent evangelist, Apollos, after a fruitful year in Corinth, joined Paul in Ephesus and brought tidings from the church in Greece.   Later messages brought news of a

less and less favorable character and disclosed distressing
conditions which had developed in the Corinthian church.
Furthermore, a delegation of three distinguished members
of the church crossed the sea to consult with the apostle.
Additional explicit information was brought him by members of the household of Chloe.

From all these sources Paul had acquired rather full
and accurate knowledge of the situation at Corinth. The
facts were in the main disturbing. The church was torn
by factions and disgracefully lax in administering discipline; the members were contending against one another
in heathen law courts and were tolerant of gross immorali-
ties in social life; they were desirous of instruction relative
to marriage, to the use of meats which had been offered to
idols, and to the proper use of spiritual gifts; they were
disorderly in their observance of the Lord's Supper, and
some were denying the doctrine of the resurrection of
the dead.

To all these conditions Paul now addresses himself with
consummate skill. Instead of answering each question by
an authoritative command or by an arbitrary rule, he states
the principle which each question involves and thus gives
a solution which is of abiding value; for while conditions
today are different from those in the Corinthian church,
the problems are analogous and to their solution the principles which Paul here sets forth can be applied. The
questions differ in form; their essence is the same and the
evangelical principles involved are of permanent validity.

Paul arranges in logical order the problems which have
been presented to him. Some readers of this letter have
taken a different view. They fail to find in this epistle
order, or method, or unity. One severe critic even ventures to say of Paul that "he had not the patience needed
for writing, he was incapable of method." On the other
hand, one of the most scholarly of modern commentators
says in referring to this letter written to the Corinthian
church, "Never was an intellectual edifice more admirably

conceived and carried out, though with the most varied materials." The subjects are, indeed, varied and heterogeneous. They are commonly listed as ten in number, including church factions, scandal, trials at law, impurity, marriage, meats offered in sacrifice, the behavior of women in public worship, the administration of the sacrament, spiritual gifts, and the resurrection of the dead.

As thus listed it will be seen that Paul treats first an ecclesiastical question, namely, the divisions in the church; then three moral questions: the case of discipline, the litigation in the law courts, and impurity in social life; then two questions of expediency, namely, marriage and the use of meats offered to idols; then three liturgical questions: the conduct of women during church service, the administration of the Lord's Supper, and the orderly exercise of spiritual gifts; and lastly a doctrinal question, namely, that of the resurrection.

The more carefully one considers the arrangement of these disconnected subjects, the more he appreciates the wisdom of the order adopted by the apostle.

In the nine verses which open the first chapter of the epistle, Paul dwells on the relation of the believer to Christ; and it is this vital relation which gives unity to the epistle, the contents of which may be thus summarized: Union with Christ is dishonored by factions (chs. 1 to 4); destroyed by impurity (chs. 5; 6); hallowed and illustrated by marriage (ch. 7); profaned by fellowship with idolatry (chs. 8 to 10); symbolized by the Lord's Supper (ch. 11); disgraced by disorder (chs. 12 to 14); consummated at the resurrection (ch. 15).

The closing chapter of the epistle gives instructions concerning the collection for the poor Christians in Jerusalem, and contains personal references and salutations. A more comprehensive and detailed outline of the epistle is presented in the following pages.

THE OUTLINE

III

I
THE SALUTATION
AND THANKSGIVING
I Cor. 1:1-9

1 Paul, called to be *an apostle of Jesus Christ through the will of God, and Sosthenes our brother, 2 unto the church of God which is at Corinth,* even *them that are sanctified in Christ Jesus, called* to be *saints, with all that call upon the name of our Lord Jesus Christ in every place, their* Lord *and ours: 3 Grace to you and peace from God our Father and the Lord Jesus Christ.*

4 I thank my God always concerning you, for the grace of God which was given you in Christ Jesus; 5 that in everything ye were enriched in him, in all utterance and all knowledge; 6 even as the testimony of Christ was confirmed in you: 7 so that ye come behind in no gift; waiting for the revelation of our Lord Jesus Christ; 8 who shall also confirm you unto the end, that ye be *unreprovable in the day of our Lord Jesus Christ. 9 God is faithful, through whom ye were called into the fellowship of his Son Jesus Christ our Lord.*

The phrases which open the epistles of Paul are of deep import. It is true that they follow the forms with which, in his day, letters usually were begun. Yet they never are empty formulas; they do much more than merely designate the writer and the readers, and extend from one to the others a conventional greeting. They are always pertinent to the letters to which they belong, and in some cases they contain almost a summary or epitome of the epistles which follow.

Thus, in the introduction of this letter, which consists of a salutation and a thanksgiving, Paul mentions the great

themes upon which he is to enlarge, namely, the unity of
the church, its purity, its spiritual gifts, and its future glory.
The first four chapters which follow are concerned with
the party divisions which were destroying Christian unity;
the next seven discuss the purity and sanctity of the church,
which were being endangered; chapters 12 to 14 treat of
the spiritual gifts with which the church was endowed;
while chapter 15 centers the thought upon the resurrection
glory which is to be enjoyed "in the day of our Lord
Jesus Christ."

Still another note is sounded by the first words of the
salutation; it is that of Paul's apostolic authority, which
certain persons were venturing to dispute. Paul therefore
begins by reminding the readers of his divine commission,
declaring that he is "an apostle of Jesus Christ" as the result of a definite call, and in accordance with "the will of
God." The summons had come to him when on his way
to Damascus, and subsequently in the city of Jerusalem;
it had reversed the course of his life and it had opened before him the vista of that worldwide testimony for Christ
to which he had been ordained by the eternal purpose of
God. The conviction of a divine vocation ever inspired
this mighty messenger of the cross, and a like conviction
should dignify and ennoble the service of the humblest follower of Christ who accepts his task, his trials, and his toils
in submission to the Master's will.

However, Paul had been summoned to no common service. He designates himself as "an apostle," by which
term he meant to claim for himself the position of an official witness, especially chosen and empowered, so that the
messages which follow were to be regarded as invested
with the very authority of Christ.

With his own name Paul associates that of Sosthenes,
whom he distinguishes not as an apostle, but as a
"brother," that is, an unofficial member of the Christian
brotherhood, who was well known by the believers in
Corinth. Their knowledge we do not share. A Sosthenes

is mentioned by the historian as being a ruler of the synagogue in Corinth, and as having been beaten by the Greeks before the judgment seat of Gallio, after Paul had been rescued by the Roman governor from the fury of the Jews. That this was the same Sosthenes, now converted from an enemy of the faith to be a follower of Christ, is a mere matter of conjecture. For this man it is enough of glory to have had his name here coupled with that of Paul; and for any one of us it is a sufficient distinction to be enrolled among the true brethren of our Lord.

The letter is addressed to "the church of God which is at Corinth." Such a designation is almost startling. It declares that the church is a divine institution; it has been established by God; it belongs to God; it is the instrument of God. Men may despise, deride, defame the church; but its origin is heavenly, its power is deathless, its destiny is glorious. In its light all nations of the earth will someday rejoice.

This church had been extended even to Corinth. That is the wonder. Even in that pagan city, amid its pride, its impurity, its absorbing rush for pleasure and for wealth, a brotherhood of believers had come into being; and never on earth has a place been found so degraded, so depraved, so morally hopeless, that the church of God cannot be established there.

This church at Corinth, Paul described as composed of them "that are sanctified in Christ Jesus," and further he spoke of the members as being "saints" as the result of a divine call. To be sanctified is to be separated from sin, and separated unto the service of God, and consequently to be pure and holy. Such persons are designated "saints," and their condition and character are attributed to the fact that they have obeyed the call to become followers of Christ. Therefore, all Christians are saints. That they are not perfectly sanctified is evident when glancing through the following chapters which describe the "saints at Corinth"; but they possess the faculty of holiness, they are being transformed by the Spirit of Christ into the likeness of Christ, and someday they are to be like him when they see him as he is.

This brotherhood of saints is confined to no one place. Paul addresses his letter not only to those at Corinth but to "all that call upon the name of our Lord Jesus Christ." Thus is sounded the note of unity which the Corinthian Christians sorely needed to heed. Their party spirit was dividing them into contending groups, and a proud self-consciousness was making them unmindful of other churches and disregardful of their practices and beliefs. Therefore, in this opening sentence of his letter, Paul assures his readers that all the Christians in Corinth formed one body of believers, and this body belonged to a universal brotherhood, composed of "all that call upon the name of our Lord Jesus Christ."

This "call" is the cry of faith which rises from the believing heart. To the call of the Spirit there has been the response of saving trust. Thus in all places and times we who belong to Christ are inseparably united with all other believers, for we acknowledge the one Lord, "their Lord and ours." Thus, too, this letter, written for the church at Corinth, is intended for us; it is designed to give warning and guidance and inspiration to all members of all churches until the end of the age.

To the universal church, and, more specifically to the saints at Corinth, Paul sends his customary and significant salutation: "Grace to you and peace from God our Father and the Lord Jesus Christ." "Grace" is a designation of the unmerited favor of God, and points to the source of all spiritual blessing; "peace" is the resultant experience of the heart which is opened by faith to receive all that God offers in and through Christ. "Grace" was a familiar salutation among the Greeks; "peace," a usual greeting among Jews; both have been united and filled with a new glory by Christians. Paul's salutation was a prayer. It well may be our petition for one another and for ourselves.

As was his custom, Paul follows his salutation by an expression of thanks. He is grateful for the grace which already has been shown to the Christians in Corinth, and specifically for the spiritual gifts by which they have been enriched, gifts, it is true, of which they have become proud, and which they have allowed to minister to their vanity. Yet these gifts were real and precious, and while later in the letter Paul is to instruct his readers as to the relative value of these endowments and is to administer a rebuke for their abuse, as he opens the letter he expresses sincere gratitude for their bestowal. By them believers have been given facility in utterance as they testified for Christ, and also a deepening "knowledge" of Christian truth, and thus by them was confirmed the testimony for Christ which Paul had borne.

So abundant was the grace thus granted that the Corinthian Christians lacked none of the spiritual gifts needed to sustain them in their life and work while they waited for the return of Christ; and Paul expresses the joyful confidence that, until the day of Christ's reappearing, the Spirit of Christ will continue to supply the needs of his followers, so that, in spite of trials and temptation, they will be "unreprovable" in "the day" of his coming. The confidence that the holiness of believers will be maintained is based not on any trust in human nature but in the faithfulness of God who has called us into fellowship with Christ. By faith we become joint partakers of his life. Therefore, as believers we should share the gratitude that Paul here expresses, rejoicing that by the Spirit of Christ every needed gift and grace will be supplied to us who belong to Christ.

We should share also in the anticipation of glory by which the Corinthian Christians were further sustained. They were "waiting for the revelation of our Lord Jesus Christ," and expecting that perfecting of spirit and of body, in the day of Christ, described by Paul in the fifteenth chapter of this epistle. This coming of Christ, this appearing in glory, should be a vital hope animating every follower of Christ.

As we look back over the introduction, it is the name of Christ which gives unity and meaning to every sentence. Nine times in the nine short verses does this name appear.

To be his apostle, Paul has been called; in fellowship with him believers are sanctified, as by calling upon him they are saved; in him, as with God the Father, grace and peace find their source; by him are bestowed the spiritual gifts which confirm the testimony of Paul and equip his fellow Christians for life and service; his return is the center of their hopes; the day of that reappearing will be the consummation of their joy; participation in his life is the essence of their experience, the explanation of their character, the assurance of their destiny.

Surely, to those who are the members of his church, Christ should become increasingly all in all.

II
THE PROBLEMS
OF THE CHURCH
Chs. 1:10 to 15:58

A. DIVISIONS   Chs. 1:10 to 4:21

1. EXHORTATION TO UNITY   Ch. 1:10-17

10 Now I beseech you, brethren, through the name of our Lord Jesus Christ, that ye all speak the same thing, and that there be no divisions among you; but that ye be perfected together in the same mind and in the same judgment. 11 For it hath been signified unto me concerning you, my brethren, by them that are of the household of Chloe, that there are contentions among you. 12 Now this I mean, that each one of you saith, I am of Paul; and I of Apollos; and I of Cephas; and I of Christ. 13 Is Christ divided? was Paul crucified for you? or were ye baptized into the name of Paul? 14 I thank God that I baptized none of you, save Crispus and Gaius; 15 lest any man should say that ye were baptized into my name. 16 And I baptized also the household of Stephanas: besides, I know not whether I baptized any other. 17 For Christ sent me not to baptize, but to preach the gospel: not in wisdom of words, lest the cross of Christ should be made void.

As Paul turns to address the church at Corinth, his first word is an exhortation to Christian unity. Possibly the first need of the modern church is this same direction. The most obvious defect in church life is its divisions: its failure to present to the world a united front, a harmonious message, or a picture of brotherhood.

This exhortation is made "through the name of our Lord Jesus Christ." The name is that "by which one is

known," or that which one is known to be. Therefore, the
name of Christ indicates all that Christ is known to be,
as Savior and Master and Lord. As all believers belong
to him, and are under his power and control, the very
mention of his name suggests an existing spiritual unity
to which outward expression should be given.

Believers should "all speak the same thing." Paul
could not have expected all Christians to unite in any one
verbal statement of their beliefs, but he besought them to
agree so far in all essentials that there would "be no divisions," no "schisms" in the body of Christ. The members
of this body should be "perfected" or "fitted together,"
having the same intellectual convictions and opinions, and
being thus united in faith and hope and love.

The occasion for such an exhortation to unity was a report which had been brought to Paul by certain relatives
or servants of Chloe, who was evidently a person of promi-
nence in the Corinthian church.

According to this report there were serious "contentions" among the Corinthian Christians. We are not to
suppose that there were separately organized parties in the
church or actual schisms from the body of believers; but
there had become manifest a divisive spirit according to
which some were renouncing their allegiance to Paul and
were declaring themselves followers of Apollos, or of Peter,
or of Christ. Just what the reasons were for such claims,
or what were the distinctions involved, are matters of mere
conjecture. Possibly those who boasted that they belonged to Paul rightfully regarded him as the founder of
the church and earnestly defended the doctrines of grace
as set forth in his simple statement of the gospel. The
followers of the gifted Alexandrian, Apollos, may have
been attracted by his philosophy and rhetoric. Those who
claimed the leadership of Cephas, or Peter, may have
done so on the ground that he was the chief apostle, or
because he was still partial to the forms and ceremonies of
Judaism. The Christ party may have protested that they

submitted to no human teachers, but built their creed on the words of Christ himself, as they interpreted these words. All these parties claimed to be Christian while more or less severely opposing their fellow believers. All have their successors in the church today.

Some are fired with evangelistic fervor; their appeal is to the emotions; they claim to preach "the simple gospel"; they are laudably eager to save souls; their range of ideas is somewhat narrow, their forms of expression are conventional, and their sympathy is rather imperfect for others whose spiritual experience is of a different type from their own; and they show scant courtesy to any who differ from them in their specific formulas of faith.

Others prefer a more philosophic statement of truth; they appeal to the intellect; they are fond of systems of theology, and enjoy abstruse speculations. Others delight in ritual; they appeal to taste and sentiment; they lay their stress on church organization; they love to trace ecclesiastical authority back to popes and apostles, even to Peter himself; to them "means of grace" are inseparable from set times and ceremonies and forms. Still others revolt from all ceremonies and all human authority; they claim to believe only in the Bible and to obey Christ alone; they wish to testify against all sects, and so form sects of their own.

All these are true Christians; there is a place for them all in the church of Christ. While human nature continues as it is, while knowledge is imperfect and tastes differ, we are hardly to expect unanimity of belief, unity in organization, or uniformity in worship. "Denominations" will continue to exist. These may work in harmony. Each may confer some temporary benefit. It is the "party spirit," expressed in rivalry and jealousy and bitterness and pride, which is to be deplored.

This is the spirit Paul rebukes by his searching question: "Is Christ divided?" If all believers belong to Christ, then all must form one body; if they are actually separated, while still holding to Christ, then Christ must be divided into several parts, which is an absurd conception.

Aside from Christ there can be no real head for any body of believers. "Was Paul crucified for you?" asks the apostle. If Christians remember who died for them, and to whom they therefore belong, they will be slow to say that they belong to Paul or Apollos or Cephas.

"Were ye baptized into the name of Paul?" It was faith in Christ, and not in any man, which they sealed and signified by baptism, and this faith brought them into a vital relation to Christ. It was denying this faith and renouncing this relation to claim such a devotion to a human leader as severed one from believers whose spiritual life had its common source in Christ.

Not only does Paul thus rebuke the party spirit, but he insists that, if it has arisen, it is not due to any fault of his own, or to the method of his ministry. He had refrained even from administering baptism, lest any might suppose that he was bringing believers into a special relationship to himself rather than into a vital fellowship with Christ. He had, indeed, baptized Crispus, the ruler of the synagogue, and Gaius, the generous benefactor of the Corinthian converts, and also "the household of Stephanas"; but so far as he could recall he had baptized no others of the great number whom he had led to Christ. He had kept in mind that the supreme task for which he had been commissioned by the Master was preaching the gospel, not even administering sacraments, however important such service might be. He realized, further, that the very character of his preaching must be such as to present clearly "the cross of Christ," and not to obscure the great fact either by the form of his message or by speculation as to its great central fact.

Christian ministers do not always realize that their supreme task is not that of administering finances, or of organizing churches, but of preaching the gospel; and they do not see that it may be possible to win for themselves followers who are not followers of Christ; they are not free from the peril of obscuring the great essential message of salvation by their very eloquence, and by their learned discussions of related themes.

2. THE GOSPEL A MANIFESTATION OF THE WISDOM AND POWER OF GOD   Ch. 1:18-31

18 For the word of the cross is to them that perish foolishness; but unto us who are saved it is the power of God. 19 For it is written,

I will destroy the wisdom of the wise,

And the discernment of the discerning will I bring to nought.

20 Where is the wise? where is the scribe? where is the disputer of this world? hath not God made foolish the wisdom of the world? 21 For seeing that in the wisdom of God the world through its wisdom knew not God, it was God's good pleasure through the foolishness of the preaching to save them that believe. 22 Seeing that Jews ask for signs, and Greeks seek after wisdom: 23 but we preach Christ crucified, unto Jews a stumblingblock, and unto Gentiles foolishness; 24 but unto them that are called, both Jews and Greeks, Christ the power of God, and the wisdom of God. 25 Because the foolishness of God is wiser than men; and the weakness of God is stronger than men.

26 For behold your calling, brethren, that not many wise after the flesh, not many mighty, not many noble, are called: *27 but God chose the foolish things of the world, that he might put to shame them that are wise; and God chose the weak things of the world, that he might put to shame the things that are strong; 28 and the base things of the world, and the things that are despised, did God choose,* yea *and the things that are not, that he might bring to nought the things that are: 29 that no flesh should glory before God. 30 But of him are ye in Christ Jesus, who was made unto us wisdom from God, and righteousness and sanctification, and redemption: 31 that, according as it is written, He that glorieth, let him glory in the Lord.*

Paul realized that the party spirit in the Corinthian church was due to a misconception of the gospel and of the Christian ministry. He therefore endeavored to rebuke and to dispel this spirit by setting forth the true nature of the gospel and of the ministry, devoting the substance of two chapters to each of these two subjects.

It is significant that today those who are seeking for "the reunion of Christendom" are endeavoring to reach a common understanding as to these identical subjects, and are holding conferences on "Faith and Order." There could be little possibility of divisions in the church if believers understood the gospel as preached by Paul and the ministry as exercised by him.

According to the apostle, the gospel was a divine revelation, manifesting the power and the wisdom of God. (Chs. 1:18 to 2:5.) Furthermore, it could be understood only when interpreted by the Spirit of God. (Chs. 2:6 to 3:4.) As such the gospel left no place for glorifying men. It was absurd for believers to say that they belonged to Paul or Apollos or Cephas or Christ, since there was but one gospel, and since it came not from men but from God.

When rebuking this foolish party spirit, Paul had declared that in preaching he had avoided any display of human learning lest he might thus obscure the essential features of the gospel. This essence he found in the doctrine of the cross of Christ.

This "word of the cross" he declared to be "foolishness" in the eyes of the reputed wise men of the world, who, however, were perishing; but to the "saved," it was manifestly "the power of God." Its divine efficacy made all human attempts to secure salvation seem foolish and futile. It had the same effect as Isaiah noted in connection with another manifestation of the power of God. Looking in pity upon the weakness of men, and about to display his own omnipotence, Jehovah was supposed by the prophet to be saying, "I will destroy the wisdom of the wise, and the discernment of the discerning will I bring to nought."

Thus in contrast with his divine gospel, God has made all the wisdom and power of man to seem absurd and impotent. "Where is the wise?" asks the apostle; "where is the scribe?" "where is the disputer of this world?" Has not God made foolish the wisdom of this world, by proclaiming the gospel of salvation through Christ?

Paul proceeds to explain how it is that the gospel has made the world's wisdom appear foolish. In his all-wise providence, God had allowed the wise men of the world to seek a way of life and a saving knowledge of God, but they had utterly failed; they "knew not God." Then in his "good pleasure," by means of the preaching of the cross, God had proceeded to save them that believed in Christ.

Therefore, when we read here of the "foolishness of . . . preaching," we are not to imagine that Paul is commending foolish preaching, nor, in fact, that he is referring to preaching as a method of propagating truth. He is referring to the substance of the message, to "the thing preached" (v. 21, margin), namely, "the cross of Christ"; it was this that seemed to be foolish in the eyes of the world. It was in reality an expression of the very wisdom of God.

Neither Jews nor Greeks are ready to receive this message, so Paul declares. Both are blinded by their own preconceptions. The "Jews ask for signs," for some strange and startling portents in the heavens, or some badges of royalty, some assumption of political power, some credentials of earthly kingship, to make them believe that the Christ who had come was the real Messiah.

The "Greeks seek after wisdom"; they believe that the way of the highest life must lie along the line of mental culture, and must follow some precepts of human philosophy. However, the apostle confidently proclaims as the only Savior. the Christ who had been crucified. Such a message is a "stumblingblock" to the Jews with their mistaken expectation of a political Messiah. It is "foolishness" to Gentiles whose confidence is placed in their own wisdom. However, to us who have accepted the call to become his followers, whether we are Jews or Greeks, Christ has become "the power of God, and the wisdom of God"; because, as a matter of fact, this divine way of salvation which seems "foolishness" to men is wiser than their wisdom, and this which seems to them "weakness" is "stronger" than any power of man.

It is not to be supposed for a moment that Paul attributes any "foolishness" to God, or that he dreams of comparing such supposed foolishness with the wisdom of men. He is speaking in irony, and is insisting that a way of salvation which men of the world regard as weak and foolish is in reality a way of divine wisdom and power.

He adds a pertinent example of the false judgments of men in this very connection. He reminds the Corinthian Christians of the world's false estimate of them, and so of the fact that God can achieve great results by means which the world despises.

"For behold your calling, brethren," writes the apostle, "that not many wise after the flesh, not many mighty, not many noble, are called: but God chose the foolish things of the world, that he might put to shame them that are wise"; for those reputed "foolish" ones found in Christ a wealth of spiritual wisdom and a saving knowledge of God which made the world's wisdom seem absolutely absurd by comparison.

So, too, God chose those whom the world regarded as weak, and gave them through faith in Christ a moral strength which made the natural power of men seem impotent by contrast. In the same way God chose men and women whom the world regarded as base, and contemptible, yes, even those who in the eyes of the world did not exist, to produce in and through them saints and martyrs and heroes who by comparison put the world to shame. This lowly origin of most of the Corinthian Christians Paul declares to be in accordance with a divine purpose, that, in the granting of salvation, no ground should be given for pride or self-satisfaction on the part of man. By the power of God, and through faith in Christ Jesus, these insignificant believers had become what they could have become by no human power or wisdom.

For them Christ had been made a "wisdom from God"; he was their Wisdom, so that in him they had treasures of knowledge and a spiritual understanding of which the world had never dreamed. Christ was their "righteousness" also; that is, in him they attained a pardon from sin and a canceling of guilt, and a peace of conscience unknown to the world. Christ was their "sanctification," for in him they found a purity and a holiness of life which the world had never attained. Christ was their "redemption," for he not only paid "the price of sin," but he rose from the dead and gave promise to his followers of a redemption which ultimately would include the body as well as the soul. In view of such a salvation secured by divine grace, and putting to shame all the wisdom of the world, Paul may well conclude with a familiar quotation: "He that glorieth, let him glory in the Lord."

All this, however, bears directly upon Paul's rebuke of the party spirit at Corinth. If the salvation was so entirely a provision of God, and if the gospel was so peculiarly a message and revelation of divine grace, where was there any excuse for division in the church, or for saying, "I am of Paul," or "I of Apollos"? Why should believers glory in men? A true knowledge of the gospel makes sectarianism seem absurd, and makes believers one in Christ.

3. PAUL'S METHOD OF PROCLAIMING THE GOSPEL
Ch. 2:1-5

1 And I, brethren, when I came unto you, came not with excellency of speech or of wisdom, proclaiming to you the testimony of God. 2 For I determined not to know anything among you, save Jesus Christ, and him crucified. 3 And I was with you in weakness, and in fear, and in much trembling. 4 And my speech and my preaching were not

in persuasive words of wisdom, but in demonstration of
the Spirit and of power: 5 that your faith should not
stand in the wisdom of men, but in the power of God.

If the church at Corinth was rent by a spirit of schism
and faction—if some were saying, "I am of Paul"; others,
"I am of Apollos" or "I am of Cephas" or "I am of
Christ"—Paul insists that the fault was not his own. In
the preceding chapter he called to mind the fact that he
had refrained from administering baptism lest any might
suppose that they were to become followers of Paul or to
belong to the church of Paul. Here he declares that even
in his mode of preaching he had given no occasion for any
persons to boast of Paul as their leader. The gospel was
a divine message; if so understood, a party spirit could
never arise in the church; and Paul had been careful so to
preach that by no display of human wisdom he should
obscure the divine character and source of his message.
He had displayed among the Corinthians no tricks of ora-
tory, no flights of eloquence, no pretensions of philosophy, in giving them his testimony of the saving grace of
God in Christ Jesus.

His task had been plain, his purpose definite; he determined to know nothing among them but Jesus Christ, and
to know and proclaim him in a way least acceptable to
the wisdom of the world, namely, as reduced to the deep
disgrace of death by the cross. It was Christ and his
atoning work and not any human philosophy of salvation
that formed the sum and substance of Paul's message.

As Paul sets forth this as his purpose when coming to
Corinth, there are some who conclude that he is confessing
that he had a different purpose when he came to Athens,
the place of his preceding ministry. It is insisted that his
ministry in Athens had been a failure, and this because he
had kept in mind and had mentioned the Greek poets and
wise men; it is said that he failed because, in his address
on Mars Hill, he had been too philosophic. This, how-

ever, is to misunderstand his message at Athens, and to misinterpret his present words to the Corinthian church.

Paul did preach Christ at Athens. His approach was conciliatory and wise, and he set forth the claims of his risen Lord with eloquence, fidelity, and power; his message was perfectly adapted to his hearers. If he met with any failure, it was due to no fault upon his part but to the intellectual pride of the hearers.

The contrast here is not between Paul's message at Athens and his preaching at Corinth but between his own preaching at Corinth and the preaching of other teachers who had been more philosophic in their discussions and who had led the auditors to think so much of the messengers that they declared themselves their followers, instead of claiming to be followers of Christ. It was this very peril that Paul avoided by the simplicity of his speech and the plainness of his preaching.

He had been with them "in weakness," by which he may have referred to that humiliating bodily infirmity which was so sore a trial to the great apostle; or he may have been recalling the mental distress and spiritual depression, as well as the "fear" and "much trembling" which made his first appearing in Corinth an experience of unparalleled distress. He had been alone in the great city, hoping for the arrival of his co-workers, Silas and Timothy; he was depressed by the surrounding mass of dense heathenism, discouraged by the pride and self-sufficiency of the Corinthians, repelled by their impurities and moral corruption, and saddened by the bitter and blasphemous opposition of his own Jewish fellow countrymen.

Then it was that he was granted, in the night, a vision of his Lord, and heard him say, "Be not afraid, but speak and hold not thy peace: for I am with thee, and no man shall set on thee to harm thee: for I have much people in this city." With this vision came a new dependence upon Christ. He spoke with no confidence in himself or in the form of his message. His "speech" and his "preaching" were not with the "persuasive words" of human "wisdom"; yet they were attended by the demonstration and the power of the Holy Spirit; and this was in accordance with the divine purpose that their faith should not be based upon any form or expression of human wisdom but on the manifested power of God.

How absurd and how sinful, then, were the party divisions in the church, which were occasioned by preferences for human teachers and by proud admiration of the gifts and cleverness of men.

The gospel is a divine message which centers in Christ, and that, too, in a Christ who has been crucified. Divisions among Christians might be healed if believers would fix their thoughts more upon their divine Lord and his redeeming grace, and would think less of the speculations and theories and formulas of men.

Then, too, in the very method of proclaiming this gospel, Christian ministers must be careful as to proportion and emphasis, as well as to form of expression, so that it can be true of them that their essential message is "Jesus Christ, and him crucified."

4. THE GOSPEL INTERPRETED ONLY BY THE SPIRIT OF GOD   Ch. 2:6-16

6 *We speak wisdom, however, among them that are full-grown: yet a wisdom not of this world, nor of the rulers of this world, who are coming to nought:* 7 *but we speak God's wisdom in a mystery, even the wisdom that hath been hidden, which God foreordained before the worlds unto our glory:* 8 *which none of the rulers of this world hath known: for had they known it, they would not have crucified the Lord of glory:* 9 *but as it is written,*

> *Things which eye saw not, and ear heard not,*
> *And which entered not into the heart of man,*
> *Whatsoever things God prepared for them that love him.*

10 *But unto us God revealed them through the Spirit:*

*for the Spirit searcheth all things, yea, the deep things of
God. 11 For who among men knoweth the things of a
man, save the spirit of the man, which is in him? even so
the things of God none knoweth, save the Spirit of God.
12 But we received, not the spirit of the world, but the
spirit which is from God; that we might know the things
that were freely given to us of God. 13 Which things also
we speak, not in words which man's wisdom teacheth, but
which the Spirit teacheth; combining spiritual things with
spiritual words. 14 Now the natural man receiveth not the
things of the Spirit of God: for they are foolishness unto
him; and he cannot know them, because they are spiritually
judged. 15 But he that is spiritual judgeth all things, and
he himself is judged of no man. 16 For who hath known
the mind of the Lord, that he should instruct him? But
we have the mind of Christ.*

Men sometimes speak of "the simple gospel." The expression is proper enough if by it they wish to describe
the Christian message when free from all human admix-
tures and corruptions. However, in a truer sense, the
gospel is anything but simple. It involves the most profound philosophy which has ever been presented to the
intellect of man. It comes directly from the mind and
heart of God. It is so subtle, so mysterious, it so far surpasses the most exalted creations of human reason, that
it cannot be understood or appreciated by men unless they
are aided by the Spirit of God.

Thus Paul affirms that, while the gospel may seem
"foolishness" to men, and while in proclaiming the gospel
he had avoided forms of human philosophy and all display
of human wisdom, nevertheless, his message was in reality
a "wisdom" which was recognized as such by those who
were "fullgrown" or spiritually matured. It was, however,
"a wisdom not of this world, nor of the rulers of this
world," who were "coming to nought," as their reputed
wisdom was being discredited by their moral impotence
and by the manifested power of the gospel. It was in

reality "God's wisdom," which Paul was proclaiming. It was "in a mystery," in the New Testament sense of that word, which indicates, not something impossible to be understood, but something which human reason never could have discovered and something the Spirit of God has made perfectly plain. Paul here definitely describes this mystery as "the wisdom that hath been hidden" (v. 7), the contents of which God has revealed to us "through the Spirit."

This wisdom, even the eternal plan of salvation through Christ, had been hidden from man; none of the intellectual or political princes of the world had discovered it, "for had they known it, they would not have crucified the Lord of glory." The men of Christ's day had no real spiritual vision; they did not understand true virtue and holiness, they could not appreciate divine love, for all these were embodied in the Savior whom they rejected and crucified. The way of salvation which God, in his grace, had prepared was one which man had not discovered and could not discover save as it was revealed to him by the Spirit of God.

Paul strengthens this statement by a quotation from Isaiah. He does not employ the very words, but states the main thought, which emphasizes the inability of man to discover that which God alone can reveal:

"Things which eye saw not, and ear heard not,
 And which entered not into the heart of man,
 Whatsoever things God prepared for them that love him."

These words do not refer to the unknown glories of heaven, as commonly is supposed, but to the way of salvation which God has prepared by the life and death and resurrection and saving power of Christ. Such a way of salvation no human eye has discovered, no human ear has heard spoken, no human heart has ever conceived. It is divine in its origin, and issues from the mind of God. It does not concern merely a future state of existence; it is a matter of present knowledge and experience; for Paul adds, "But unto us God revealed them through the Spirit: for the Spirit searcheth all things, yea, the deep things of God."

Thus the gospel is not only divine in its origin but so divine in its nature that it can be understood only by the aid of the Spirit of God.

When it is said that the Spirit searcheth all things, the word is not to be understood as implying a partial knowledge, needing to be made complete, but a deep and accurate knowledge already possessed, as when reference is made to God as the Searcher of hearts. This knowledge Paul compares to the self-consciousness of men. None but a man's own spirit can know what passes in his breast, or dwells in his mind and heart; so none but the Spirit of God can understand the deep purposes and plans and wisdom of God, such purposes and plans and wisdom indeed as are embodied in the gospel of Christ. In order that Christians may understand this gospel, Paul claims, God gives them an illumination differing from the intelligence of the wise men of the world, a certain spiritual discernment which can be traced to the direct influence of the Spirit of God; this Spirit is imparted to us in order that we may be able to comprehend the message of grace so "freely given to us of God."

This message, Paul declares, he has been setting forth, "not in words which man's wisdom teacheth, but which the Spirit teacheth; combining spiritual things with spiritual words." By the last phrase Paul may mean "interpreting spiritual things to spiritual men" or "setting forth spiritual truths with Spirit-given words."

It is not strange, therefore, that the gospel seems mere foolishness to men of the world, to "natural" men, unspiritual men, whose perceptions do not extend beyond the sphere of the intellect; for the gospel is concerned with truths which belong to the realm of the spirit, and can be understood only by "spiritual" men. By the word "spirit"

Paul here means the human spirit when influenced by the Spirit of God, and by spiritual men he denotes those who are under the control of the Spirit of God. It is evident then why "the natural man receiveth not the things of the Spirit of God," and why "they are foolishness unto him," and why he "cannot know them"; it is "because they are spiritually judged" or spiritually examined. The unbelieving man, the "natural man," the man who is not illumined by the Spirit of Christ, is not qualified even to examine or scrutinize, much less to comprehend, the gospel. On the other hand, "he that is spiritual judgeth all things," even the very things which human eye has not discerned, or human ear heard, or human mind conceived, even the deep things of God. He may be uncultured according to worldly standards, or dull and stupid in the estimation of men, but he can apprehend truths which the wisest and keenest natural man cannot perceive; and to the natural man he is a mystery. No man of the world can understand a Christian; he "is judged of no man."

On the other hand, we who have accepted the gospel, we who have been illumined by the Spirit, "we have the mind of Christ." This does not mean that a Christian claims to have a moral temper as perfect as that of his Master, nor does it mean that his knowledge is superhuman, but it does mean that under the influence of the Holy Spirit his moral and intellectual faculties are so quickened and enlightened that he can understand the way of salvation proclaimed by Christ, wrought out by Christ, approved by Christ, and made plain to men by the Spirit of Christ.

Therefore, if the gospel is thus divine in its origin and its nature, why should Christians who accept this gospel allow themselves to be divided into parties by the men who proclaim this gospel? If they are true to their one message, these men will agree; and if they are faithful in their ministry, they will not obscure their gospel by human devices and rhetoric and philosophy. When Christians are so illumined by the Spirit of Christ that they can understand the gospel of Christ, then divisions in the church will cease.

5. PARTISANSHIP, A PROOF OF SPIRITUAL IMMATURITY   Ch. 3:1-4

1 And I, brethren, could not speak unto you as unto spiritual, but as unto carnal, as unto babes in Christ. 2 I fed you with milk, not with meat; for ye were not yet able to bear it: *nay, not even now are ye able; 3 for ye are yet carnal: for whereas there is among you jealousy and strife, are ye not carnal, and do ye not walk after the manner of men?   4 For when one saith, I am of Paul; and another, I am of Apollos; are ye not men?*

Nothing could be more childish in Christians or more indicative of low spiritual life than divisions, and denominational rivalries, and factions.   Thus when Paul is rebuking the members of the Corinthian church for their party spirit, he tells them that they are showing themselves to be mere "babes in Christ" and are acting like the unregenerate men of the world.

It was a sharp home thrust, for the Corinthians prided themselves on their spiritual gifts and attainments, and Paul's critics had sneered at the simplicity of his teaching. The apostle retorts that this simplicity was due to their immaturity. He had merely adapted himself to their incapacity. As a spiritual man he "could not speak" to them as to spiritual men, simply for the reason that they would not have been able to understand or to accept such teaching. "The natural man receiveth not the things of the Spirit of God: for they are foolishness unto him; and he cannot know them, because they are spiritually judged."

Paul does not mean that the Corinthians were not Christians, but that he had found them in a state of spiritual infancy. They had experienced a new birth, but the old nature and disposition were hindering in them the action of the Spirit. They were undeveloped. They were "babes in Christ."

There is no disgrace in being a babe, but prolonged infancy is pitiable, and arrested development is deplorable. Regeneration does not denote moral perfection, but the beginning of a new life. There must be growth from the state of a babe to that of a mature man.

Paul had realized the condition of the Corinthian Christians, and because of their spiritual immaturity he had fed them "with milk, not with meat." He had given them food adapted to babes. He had taught them only the more simple truths of the gospel. He saw that they were not able to receive and assimilate solid food, in the form of more difficult doctrines and more advanced spiritual teachings. He had preached "Jesus Christ, and him crucified," but had confined himself to only the more elementary forms and simpler applications of the gospel message.

There is a proper time and place for such preaching. All persons need to learn of the pardon and peace and power which result from faith in the crucified and risen Christ. To accept this Christ as Lord and Master and to experience a new birth is to begin a new life.

Justly to appreciate these truths, to live by them, and to apply them to our every need is to develop spiritually, and to be able to receive and appreciate more advanced forms of Christian teaching.

This the Corinthians had failed to do. They were still undeveloped, still mere babes in Christ, still unable to digest solid food. They were still "carnal," in a state where the "flesh" overpowered the spirit, where the old nature and disposition controlled the new. They were seen to "walk after the manner of men," to live as those who had not been given a new life by the Spirit of God but were still unregenerate men of the world.

The proof of this immature, undeveloped, worldly state was found in their envying and strife and divisions: "For when one saith, I am of Paul; and another, I am of Apollos; are ye not men?" The mere fact that divisions existed among the Corinthian Christians was proof of their spiritual immaturity, but the envy and strife which caused and exaggerated their divisions were further indications of their undeveloped and carnal state.

Many Christians pride themselves on belonging to a certain party in the church, whereas the very existence of the party may be a disgrace, and the spirit of faction in which the party had its rise may demonstrate a pitiful failure to understand the gospel of Christ.

Mature Christians, "spiritual" Christians, rejoice in the unity of the church. To them the Spirit of God has revealed the deeper things of God and made them feel that they are one with all the children of God. They seek to maintain and to manifest the oneness which the Spirit gives, in the bonds of peace, "till we all attain unto the unity of the faith, and of the knowledge of the Son of God, unto a fullgrown man, unto the measure of the stature of the fulness of Christ."

6. CHRISTIAN MINISTERS ARE SERVANTS OF GOD, NOT MASTERS OF MEN   Ch. 3:5-9

5 What then is Apollos? and what is Paul? Ministers through whom ye believed; and each as the Lord gave to him. 6 I planted, Apollos watered; but God gave the increase. 7 So then neither is he that planteth anything, neither he that watereth; but God that giveth the increase. 8 Now he that planteth and he that watereth are one: but each shall receive his own reward according to his own labor. 9 For we are God's fellow-workers: ye are God's husbandry, God's building.

Paul has been showing that the party spirit in the church would be corrected by a true view of the gospel as a message from God revealed by the Spirit of God. Such a conception would make it impossible to glory in men or to divide the church into factions which boasted of the various messages delivered by men.

He now proceeds to show that such a spirit of division

would be restrained further by a right view of Christian
ministers as being servants of God, and not masters
of men.

The word "minister" is in itself beautiful and suggestive.
It means a "servant," and is so used in the New Testament. It never means the pastor of a church or the head
of a congregation, as it commonly does in modern speech.
Paul declares that he and Apollos and other gospel messengers are merely servants belonging to God, and that it
is absurd for the Christians at Corinth to divide into parties, saying that they belong to men whom God has sent
to serve them. The gospel messengers belong to God.
Those who have received the message belong to God, and
should be thankful to God for the service his messengers
have rendered. Thy should not be proud or envious because of the various benefits his workmen have bestowed.
Such a true view of the Christian ministry would unite
believers in common gratitude, not divide them by a spirit
of rivalry and faction.

"What then is Apollos?" the writer asks of his Corinthian readers, "and what is Paul?" Surely they have not
come as leaders of parties, as founders of sects, as lords
over Christian believers. They are servants of God who
have come to form and to strengthen a united church composed of all the followers of Christ. They are "ministers
through whom ye believed." Each one has performed a
task which the Lord assigned. Paul has done the planting;
Apollos has done the watering; but it is God who has
made the plant to grow. The work has been begun, indeed, by Paul, and it has been continued by Apollos, but
for neither should superior credit be claimed, as God
alone has given prosperity to both. "So then neither is he
that planteth anything, neither he that watereth." They
are nothing in themselves or of themselves, or in comparison with God, for it is "God that giveth the increase."

These servants, Paul and Apollos, are not rivals. They
should not be regarded as leaders of sects. They have

different tasks, but they are united in their aim and purpose. "He that planteth and he that watereth are one." Their common interest is the advancement of the church. They are cooperating, not competing.

Insofar as their opportunities and responsibilities differ, they will receive each one his proper wage in accordance with the effort he has put forth, and proportionate to his fidelity to his task: "Each shall receive his own reward according to his own labor."

Believers, too, should not regard themselves as belonging to these laborers, nor boast that they are followers of one rather than another in view of some imagined superiority of one task over another. Such a spirit of division is wholly unwarranted for "we" Christian ministers, "we" gospel messengers, "we" servants of the church "are God's fellow-workers." We are not workers with God. That is not the idea the apostle is here setting forth. We are fellow workers who belong to God, and who are working with one another. As God's servants we have a common task; it is to labor in the field which belongs to God, in the church, in the tilled land where one has been doing the planting and another the watering; or, suddenly to change the figure of speech, we are fellow workers engaged in erecting the great temple which is being built for a habitation of God. "For," writes the apostle, while "we are God's fellow-workers: ye are God's husbandry, God's building."

Such a conception of the Christian ministry will secure unity for the church and promote humility and sympathy among the servants of Christ.

7. THE RESPONSIBILITY OF THE CHRISTIAN MINISTRY   Ch. 3:10-17

10 According to the grace of God which was given unto me, as a wise masterbuilder I laid a foundation; and another buildeth thereon. But let each man take heed how

*he buildeth thereon. 11 For other foundation can no man
lay than that which is laid, which is Jesus Christ.   12 But
if any man buildeth on the foundation gold, silver, costly
stones, wood, hay, stubble;   13 each man's work shall be
made manifest: for the day shall declare it, because it is
revealed in fire; and the fire itself shall prove each man's
work of what sort it is.   14 If any man's work shall abide
which he built thereon, he shall receive a reward.   15 If
any man's work shall be burned, he shall suffer loss: but
he himself shall be saved; yet so as through fire.*

*16 Know ye not that ye are a temple of God, and that
the Spirit of God dwelleth in you?   17 If any man destroyeth the temple of God, him shall God destroy; for the temple of God is holy, and such are ye.*

While various forms of service are allotted to different
servants of Christ, each is responsible for the quality of his
work.   These forms are depicted by Paul in speaking of
the church as a field in which his task had been to plant
and that of Apollos to water, the rising grain.

However, better to suit his purpose, Paul changes the
figure from that of a field to that of a temple.   Christian
ministers are fellow workmen.   Each has a different part
in the building, and each is responsible for the materials
he employs and for the work he does.   Everyone should
strive so to build that his construction will stand the test
of Christ's judgment and will merit a reward.

As for himself, Paul declares that he has acted as a wise
master builder.   He guards against seeming to be proud
and presumptuous by asserting that his wisdom was due
to "the grace of God" which had been given him, and,
therefore, the merit is not his own.   He had "laid a
foundation."   He had begun the church at Corinth, and
all that other teachers were doing was to build on the
foundation he had laid.   These teachers should take heed
to the character of their building.   One thing was certain:
whatever their work might be, they could lay no other
foundation.   For the Foundation he had laid was Jesus
Christ.   Paul had established the church at Corinth by

proclaiming his crucified, his risen, his coming Lord. Indeed God himself had laid this Foundation for the church,
so that in very truth "other foundation can no man lay
than that which is laid, which is Jesus Christ."

Nevertheless, it is possible to build upon this foundation
structures of various materials. One minister may build
with durable and rich materials, such as gold and silver
and precious stones. Another may employ those which
are perishable and paltry, like wood or hay or stubble.
Exactly what in the mind of Paul corresponded to these
various materials is not quite certain. Some think he referred to true or false doctrines. Others suppose that Paul
had reference here to persons, some good and some worthless, who are brought into the visible church of Christ.
Still others believe that the apostle referred to the moral
and spiritual fruits of the work of Christian teachers in the
lives and characters of their disciples and followers. These
three views are not necessarily discrepant or mutually ex-
clusive. Sound doctrines do mold character and determine
conduct, while worthless, foolish, and false teaching does
result in merely empty professions of faith, and in building
up churches which seem large and strong, but which cannot stand the test of time or the judgment of Christ.

Such a day of testing and disclosure is certain to come.
"Each man's work shall be made manifest" in its true
character. "The day" of Christ's return "shall declare it,"
that future glorious day when he will come and reward his
servants. His judgment will be like a fire testing the true
value of the work each man has done. Some work will
be found to have been worthless and vain, and some will
prove to be of abiding value. Each man whose work is
approved shall receive a reward; each one whose work
fails to stand the fiery test of divine judgment shall lose his
reward. He may not lose his soul. If he has been building upon Christ as a foundation, he may be saved even
though his work perishes.

However, he will be like one who escapes from a burning building. "He himself shall be saved; yet so as through

fire." This expression has become proverbial in describing a narrow and perilous escape. It may also picture the burning sense of shame and disillusionment and remorse which will be felt by a Christian minister whose apparently successful work is found at last to have been flimsy and worthless and tawdry and unreal.

All this bears directly upon the theme with which Paul is opening the epistle, namely, the divisions in the church at Corinth. It contains practical messages for the church of today. First, if there is and can be but one Foundation, then all persons who are united with Christ belong to the one building. There can be but one Christian church. Parties and sects are unnatural and inconsistent with a true dependence upon Christ.

Secondly, if Paul founded the church by preaching nothing but "Christ, and him crucified," then for members of the church to proclaim themselves followers of some other teacher is to turn away not only from Paul but from the Christ he preached. To repudiate Paul is to abandon Christ.

In the third place, while some teachers may enjoy great popularity and while their followers may make for their work extravagant claims, the real test of service is not the praise of men but the judgment of Christ. Some of the very leaders who are being lauded at the expense of Paul may be disappointed in the day of Christ's coming; they may not be lost, but they may be denied any reward.

Paul not unnaturally closes the paragraph with a solemn warning. Divisions may injure, they may defile, they may destroy the sanctuary of God, his inviolable temple, the church of Jesus Christ. This temple is formed of believers, as of living stones. It rests upon the divine Son of God, and is indwelt by the Spirit of God. If by a spirit of faction, if by pride and vanity, a man causes divisions in the church, he will suffer the punishment of God. "If any man destroyeth the temple of God, him shall God destroy; for the temple of God is holy, and such are ye."

8. THE FOLLY OF CHURCH FACTIONS   Ch. 3:18-23

18 Let no man deceive himself. If any man thinketh that he is wise among you in this world, let him become a fool, that he may become wise. 19 For the wisdom of this world is foolishness with God. For it is written, He that taketh the wise in their craftiness: 20 and again, The Lord knoweth the reasonings of the wise, that they are vain. 21 Wherefore let no one glory in men. For all things are yours; 22 whether Paul, or Apollos, or Cephas, or the world, or life, or death; or things present, or things to come; all are yours; 23 and ye are Christ's; and Christ is God's.

Those who cause divisions in the church are usually moved by vanity and pride. In any case, they are guilty of folly, for they assume superiority to other Christians, and defraud their own followers by depriving them of instruction which other leaders are able to give, and which belongs in common to all who are disciples of Christ.

Such is the contention of the apostle as he continues to rebuke the Corinthians for their spirit of faction and to insist that this would be cured in large measure by a true view of Christian ministers as all being servants of the whole church and not belonging to separate sects.

"Let no man deceive himself," writes Paul. None should pride himself on possessing any superior wisdom as to the way of salvation, or as to a true knowledge of God. It is found only in the gospel of Christ, and in the preaching of the cross. This message seems foolish to the wise men of the world, as the apostle has shown in the first chapter of the epistle; but it is in reality the very wisdom of God.

Therefore, the apostle insists, whoever of you regards himself as wise with wisdom of this age must become a fool in the eyes of the world, by accepting the gospel of Christ, and thus becoming truly wise. "For the wisdom of this world is foolishness with God."

This fact is established by the words of Job, "He taketh the wise in their own craftiness," where the reference is to the futility of human wisdom, and its inability to reach the ends at which it aims. It is further established by the words of the psalmist, "The Lord knoweth the reasonings of the wise, that they are vain," where the reference is to the emptiness, the vanity, of human wisdom, not merely as to its result but as to its very essence.

It must be understood that Paul is here estimating human wisdom only from the viewpoint of its inability to discover and attain salvation. All the truths of science and philosophy, all advances in every sphere of human knowledge, are to be prized and to be received with gratitude as the gifts of God to men; but the gospel of salvation is a divine wisdom and superior to all the philosophies of earth. It came from the mind of God; it concerns the Son of God; it is revealed by the Spirit of God.

"Wherefore let no one glory in men." Cease your proud and selfish boastings through your preference for one or another Christian teacher. Do not "glory in men"; do not take honor from belonging to them as your masters; they really belong to you as your servants. Remember that "all are yours" if you belong to Christ.

Then Paul specifies some of these "things," and gives what has been called an "inventory of the possessions of the child of God."

Christian ministers are yours: Paul, with his unique knowledge of the gospel message and with his matchless missionary zeal and fervor; Apollos, with his profound knowledge of the Scriptures and his moving eloquence; Peter, with his personal memories of the Lord. All these are yours. Do not say that you belong to them. Say that they belong to you. And since they belong to you they belong to all Christians alike. Do not impoverish yourselves; do not defraud the church by your divisions. You all have a right not only to what you derive from your favorite teacher but to what you may derive from all the teachers. Every truth taught by any Christian minister belongs to the whole church of Christ.

Paul and Apollos and Cephas are yours. Therefore the church which these leaders represent is yours; but so is the "world." The whole existing order of material things is yours. It is for you to enjoy. It is being ordered for your benefit. Do not think that the world is against you. All its treasures of beauty and mystery and light are yours. "To them that love God all things work together for good."

Life and death are yours. It is Christ alone who can give meaning to life, and make it worth living. It is foolish to deny the reality of pain and disappointment and sorrow. These are bitter and baffling and cruel; yet out of them issues some abiding good, here or hereafter. For death is yours. He is your servant even when he seems to over-master you. His livery is black; his accompaniments are those of terror and dread; but someday you shall see him draw aside the curtain and usher you into another life radiant with glory and with joy. "Things present, or things to come" are also yours. Not only all states of being but all periods and possibilities of time belong to the Christian. For him Christ fills the present with victory and the future with hope.

"All are yours," repeats the apostle; but he at once adds, "All are yours" only in case and on condition that "ye are Christ's." If he is indeed your Master and Lord, then nothing can harm you permanently, nothing can be against you; all things will help you, all things will serve you, all things will be for you, all on your side, all in your favor; for "ye are Christ's; and Christ is God's."

The church possesses all things in view of the fact that it is subject to Christ and depends upon Christ who is Ruler of all things; and Christ himself has such universal power because he is subject to God and depends upon God.

This submission of the Son to the Father does not raise the question of his true deity. It rather is a truth which enables us to conceive the unity in the divine Trinity. The universal sovereignty of the Son of God rests upon his filial subjection to the Father. So the unity and sanctity and grandeur of the church rest upon its submission and obedience to Christ. As servants of Christ we become heirs of all things.

In view of such relations how can the church allow itself to be divided? How can one glory in himself, or in his subjection to a human teacher? Each believer possesses "all things," including the very teachers who have been sent as his servants. His glory, his boasting, his riches, are in Christ, in whom all believers share a common blessedness and dignity and life.

9. CHRISTIAN MINISTERS ANSWERABLE TO GOD
Ch. 4:1-5

1 Let a man so account of us, as of ministers of Christ, and stewards of the mysteries of God. 2 Here, moreover, it is required in stewards, that a man be found faithful. 3 But with me it is a very small thing that I should be judged of you, or of man's judgment: yea, I judge not mine own self. 4 For I know nothing against myself; yet am I not hereby justified: but he that judgeth me is the Lord. 5 Wherefore judge nothing before the time, until the Lord come, who will both bring to light the hidden things of darkness, and make manifest the counsels of the hearts; and then shall each man have his praise from God.

It is hard to be misjudged, to be condemned when doing one's best, and to see others receive praise which they do not deserve. This very injustice was being done to Paul by the party spirit in the Corinthian church, and by the partiality which the members were showing toward certain teachers. This partisanship not only injured the church and defrauded its members, as the apostle has just shown, but it wronged the ministers who had been given to the church as its servants. While they were indeed the servants of the church, it was not their master. They were the servants of God and were answerable to him. Therefore they should not have been subjected to unkind criticisms, and made the occasion of the needless divisions which were doing such harm to the church.

Thus Paul continues to rebuke the partisan spirit among the Corinthian Christians. In doing so, however, he does exactly what he has done in the opening of each of the two preceding chapters. In all three cases he applies to his own personal relation with the church at Corinth the truths he has previously established.

Here, after discussing the position of Christian ministers as servants of the church, he turns to consider the Christian teachers at Corinth, and more specifically his own case and experience, in relation to the church.

"Let a man so account of us, as of ministers of Christ." We are indeed sent to serve the church; yet the church is not to judge and condemn us, to choose among us, to accept or to reject us, as though it were our master. We are servants of Christ, his assistants and helpers. And we are "stewards of the mysteries of God." The word "steward" was employed to denote "a confidential slave to whom a master entrusted the direction of his house, and in particular the care of distributing to all the servants their tasks and provisions." Thus Christian ministers are dispensers and administrators of divine truths. They must render an account, therefore, not to their fellow servants but to God.

They go where they are sent and share what has been revealed to them. Faithfulness to their Master and to their mission is all that can be required of them.

To accept one of these stewards and to reject another is to imply that one is more faithful than the other, and is thus to take the place of a judge, which belongs to the Lord alone.

In view of this Judge, Paul declares himself but little concerned with the opinions of other men. "With me it is a very small thing that I should be judged of you, or of man's judgment." It is even of as little consequence to Paul what estimate he places upon himself. While he is not aware of any unfaithfulness to his stewardship, yet the approval of his own conscience is not a just ground of complacency, nor does he for that reason stand acquitted. The One whose scrutiny he must undergo, the One as to whose judgment he is concerned, is the Lord.

Therefore Paul urges the Corinthians to cease from the premature and officious judgment of their teachers which has resulted in schism and faction. When the Lord comes he "will . . . bring to light" the hidden acts of life and will reveal the secret motives of men's hearts. Then the praise which each man deserves will come to him, not from ignorant and impertinent partisans, but from God, the just and infallible Judge.

These are words of wise counsel. Let us be slow and humble in judging our fellowmen, particularly in assuming to know the motives of Christian ministers. Let us not be envious or discouraged in accomplishing our given tasks, but seek only to be faithful in all things. Let us not be too much teased and tormented by the opinions and judgments of others. A day of vindication is coming; "The Lord is at hand."

10. PRIDE, THE SOURCE OF FACTION, REPROVED
Ch. 4:6-13

6 Now these things, brethren, I have in a figure trans-ferred to myself and Apollos for your sakes; that in us ye might learn not to go *beyond the things which are written; that no one of you be puffed up for the one against the other. 7 For who maketh thee to differ? and what hast thou that thou didst not receive? but if thou didst receive it, why dost thou glory as if thou hadst not received it? 8 Already are ye filled, already ye are become rich, ye have come to reign without us: yea and I would that ye did reign, that we also might reign with you. 9 For, I think, God hath set forth us the apostles last of all, as men doomed to death: for we are made a spectacle unto the world, both to angels and men. 10 We are fools for Christ's sake, but ye are wise in Christ; we are weak, but ye are strong; ye have glory, but we have dishonor. 11 Even unto this present hour we both hunger, and thirst, and are naked, and are buffeted, and have no certain dwelling-place; 12 and we toil, working with our on hands: being reviled, we bless; being persecuted, we endure; 13 being defamed, we entreat: we are made as the filth of the world, the offscouring of all things, even until now.*

More than once Paul has intimated that the divisions in the Corinthian church were the result and evidence of vanity and pride. Here he rebukes this foolish complacency by contrasting his own experience as an apostle with the glorying and boasting and self-satisfaction of the Corinthians. They were acting as though already in the full enjoyment of the future perfected Kingdom of Christ; and Paul, meanwhile, like a gladiator in the arena, condemned to death, was suffering the extreme of obloquy and anguish and torment and disgrace.

"Now these things, brethren," that is, all that has been said as to the folly of factions and divisions, "I have in a figure transferred to myself and Apollos," although the principles are of wider application and refer to your attitude toward all your teachers; and I have not been speaking in self-defense, but "for your sakes." I have been endeavoring to teach you a lesson of humility, "that in us," by our example and by my insisting on your right attitude toward us "ye might learn not to go beyond the things which are written" in the Scriptures. Paul has in view no specific passages, but the general teaching of Scripture as to the folly of conceit and self-sufficiency. He would have the Corinthian Christians avoid the pride and partisanship connected with preferences for individual teachers, "that no one of you be puffed up for the one against the other," taking sides of boasted rivalry, exalting one teacher to the disparagement of another.

Such an exaltation of their teachers was, in their case, not an act of loyalty or of grateful homage; it was a gratification of their pride. The party divisions were ministering to their vanity.

Moreover, they were presumptuous and unnecessary: "For who maketh thee to differ?" The separation between a believer and his fellows has been made by himself. He has chosen some special leader and needlessly, foolishly, allied himself with some party.

Such a separation is ungrateful: "What hast thou that thou didst not receive?" The very excellencies which were the grounds of division were the gifts of God. They were occasions for gratitude, not for pride. They should not minister to self-glory, as though they had been gained and not given.

Yet the conceit of the Corinthians was boundless. Paul pictures it with bitter irony. "Already are ye filled," as men who even now have attained to your estate in the future Kingdom of glory. "Already ye are become rich." "Without waiting for us apostles," Paul says in substance, "you have ascended your thrones. And would that you had ascended thrones, for then we should be reigning with you."

In contrast with such childish fancies is the pitiful reality of the apostles' actual condition. It can be compared only with that of condemned criminals who came last into the amphitheater when the spectators had been sated with less bloody exhibitions; they were compelled to fight unarmed with wild beasts, and for them there was no hope of life. Or the apostles were like those gladiators who came into the arena knowing they would never leave it alive; they had bidden their friends farewell, and they saluted the emperor as those about to die: "For, I think, God hath set forth us the apostles last of all, as men doomed to death: for we are made a spectacle unto the world, both to angels and men."

Again Paul turns to the Corinthians with scathing sarcasm. The words were addressed particularly to the party leaders in the church but applied equally to all their followers. "We are fools for Christ's sake"; we have incurred that reproach for our loyalty to the gospel which is ever regarded as foolishness by the wise men of the world; "but ye are wise in Christ"; you have acquired a method of preaching that gospel which has won for yourselves a reputation for wisdom and understanding. "We are weak, but ye are strong"; you make your public addresses with self-confidence and assurance, but we lack your lordly airs and appear with fear and much trembling. "Ye have glory, but we have dishonor." You are received with praise and adulation; we are reviled and despised.

Upon this last pathetic contrast Paul dwells at greater length in depicting what the apostles are enduring for Christ's sake. For them life is becoming no easier as time goes on. "Even unto this present hour we both hunger, and thirst." We have little to make us imagine that the hour of triumph and coronation has come. On the other hand, we "are naked, and are buffeted, and have no certain dwelling-place; and we toil, working with our own hands."

Their conduct, however, is patient and humble. To insulting sneers they reply with blessing. They meet persecution with uncomplaining self-control. They answer calumnies by entreating men to repent and to turn to Christ.

For such conduct what do they receive but more complete contempt? "We are made as the filth of the world, the offscouring of all things, even until now."

While Paul and his fellow apostles were thus regarded by the world, it was absurd for the Corinthians to imagine that they could gain much honor by claiming to follow one rather than another of these despised leaders. While they were being thus treated, their followers could hardly be in a mood of self-complacency and boasting. The pride

which caused the factions in the Corinthian church was
senseless and stupid and heartless and absurd.

11. PAUL'S FATHERLY ADMONITION   Ch. 4:14-21

*14 I write not these things to shame you, but to admon-
ish you as my beloved children.   15 For though ye have
ten thousand tutors in Christ, yet have ye not many fathers;
for in Christ Jesus I begat you through the gospel.   16 I
beseech you therefore, be ye imitators of me.   17 For this
cause have I sent unto you Timothy, who is my beloved
and faithful child in the Lord, who shall put you in remembrance of my ways which are in Christ, even as I teach
everywhere in every church.   18 Now some are puffed
up, as though I were not coming to you.   19 But I will
come to you shortly, if the Lord will; and I will know,
not the word of them that are puffed up, but the power.
20 For the kingdom of God is not in word, but in power.
21 What will ye? shall I come unto you with a rod, or in
love and a spirit of gentleness?*

With this fatherly appeal Paul closes his long discussion.
The divisions in the church at Corinth have been his theme
in the four opening chapters of the epistle.   The matter is
so serious that in his last paragraph he has felt constrained
to adopt a tone of mingled irony and reproach.   Now with
an abrupt and sudden change, so characteristic of his style,
he turns to make a tender and sympathetic appeal.   Yet
even here a note of severity is not wanting; it rather pre-
pares for the stern demand of the chapter which will
follow.

Here Paul explains the language he has employed.   In
all he has said about the factions and divisions among the
Christians at Corinth and in his most severe rebuke, he
has been seeking their highest good.   "I write not these
things to shame you, but to admonish you as my beloved
children."   They were indeed his own.   They belonged to
him as to no other teacher or leader.   It was absurd for

them to form divisions and to say, "I am of Paul; and
I of Apollos; and I of Cephas; and I of Christ." A great
multitude of new teachers may have appeared, but though
the Corinthians might have ten thousand Christian tutors,
they had but one spiritual father, namely, Paul. In fellowship with Christ and by preaching the gospel he had imparted to them a new life. Very properly, therefore, he
entreats them to be imitators of his humility and his unselfish service, and to show their likeness to their father in
Christ by putting away the spirit of pride and faction and
conceit.

To aid them in ending their strife and divisions, he has
sent to them Timothy, his "beloved and faithful child in
the Lord." His conversion had been due to the influence
of Paul. He was, therefore, like an elder brother to the
Corinthians, and as such should be welcomed with affection and trust. His mission is to put them in remembrance
of the "ways" of Paul, his modes of action, which he taught
in all the churches, his humility and abnegation and devotion to the Lord. These Paul always practiced and these
he taught in all the churches.

His sending of Timothy must not be taken to indicate
that Paul was not coming to Corinth. Certain enemies of
the apostle seemed to have so concluded. With an air of
triumph these self-inflated partisans were proclaiming that
Timothy was coming instead of Paul. In the absence of
the apostle these mischievous teachers had swelled into
importance. Because of the fact of Timothy's coming they
were bearing themselves the more insolently; possibly they
were intimating that Paul was afraid of them. "Now
some are puffed up," writes the apostle, "as though I were
not coming to you. But I will come to you shortly, if the
Lord will; and I will know, not the word of them that are
puffed up, but the power." Paul will discover and will
show whether these conceited opponents of his have any
power corresponding to their proud pretensions and eloquent tirades. For the Kingdom of God which is to be

established, and so the apostolic service and authority by which it is being hastened, are matters not of words but of power. When Paul arrives in Corinth he will not confine himself to words and teachings and rebukes. He will act. How shall he act? This will depend altogether upon the Corinthians. If by their factions and divisions they continue to behave like foolish and disobedient children, he will chastise them; if they reveal unity and sympathy and love, he will show himself to be a gentle and forgiving father. "What will ye? shall I come unto you with a rod, or in love and a spirit of gentleness?"

Thus, in these first four chapters of his letter, Paul has sought to correct the party spirit at Corinth and to bring the Christians into a spirit of unity. It was the topic of which he needed to treat first; for only to a united church which recognized him as its founder could he address the stern commands and give the authoritative teachings which follow. In the present day, wherever there exists a spirit of suspicion and pride and faction, this spirit must first be dispelled before there can be any real advance in life or knowledge or service.

B. DISCIPLINE   Ch. 5

1 It is actually reported that there is fornication among you, and such fornication as is not even among the Gentiles, that one of you hath his father's wife. 2 And ye are puffed up, and did not rather mourn, that he that had done this deed might be taken away from among you. 3 For I verily, being absent in body but present in spirit, have already as though I were present judged him that hath so wrought this thing, 4 in the name of our Lord Jesus, ye being gathered together, and my spirit, with the power of our Lord Jesus, 5 to deliver such a one unto Satan for the destruction of the flesh, that the spirit may be saved in the day of the Lord Jesus. 6 Your glorying is not good. Know ye not that a little leaven leaveneth the whole lump? 7 Purge out the old leaven, that ye may be a new lump, even as ye are unleavened. For our passover also hath been sacrificed, even Christ: 8 wherefore let us keep the feast, not with old leaven, neither with the leaven of malice and wickedness, but with the unleavened bread of sincerity and truth.

9 I wrote unto you in my epistle to have no company with fornicators; 10 not at all meaning *with the fornicators of this world, or with the covetous and extortioners, or with idolaters; for then must ye needs go out of the world: 11 but as it is, I wrote unto you not to keep company, if any man that is named a brother be a fornicator, or covetous, or an idolater, or a reviler, or a drunkard, or an extortioner; with such a one no, not to eat. 12 For what have I to do with judging them that are without? Do not ye judge them that are within? 13 But them that are without God judgeth. Put away the wicked man from among yourselves.*

According to common rumor a case of gross immorality was being countenanced among the Christians at Corinth. Therefore, after his long discussion of the divisions in the church, Paul turns to insist that discipline be inflicted upon the offending member. While this was the most serious matter with which Paul had to deal, it could not have been treated first. Unity must be established before drastic action could be urged; otherwise the action would have been that of a party and the division in the church might have been made worse.

Then again, the administering of discipline is in a sense a matter of church life, of church organization, of church action. Therefore it is closely allied, as an ecclesiastical question, to the problem of divisions which it follows. However, it involves a serious moral fault, and properly introduces the two moral questions which follow, namely, vindictive lawsuits and personal impurity. Thus the order followed by Paul is strictly logical and the first six chapters of the epistle are bound into a close unity.

1. The Deserved Severity   Ch. 5:1-5

The fault of the offender was grievous indeed. He was living in immoral relations with his stepmother. Such a crime would not have been tolerated even by pagans, with their lower standards of morality. Yet the Christians at Corinth, indifferent to the scandal, were still boasting of their rival leaders, still filled with self-complacent pride. They should have been overwhelmed with shame, and should have shut out of their communion the one who had brought upon them such disgrace.

They should have understood that the true glory of the Christian church consists not in the eloquence and gifts of its great teachers but in the moral purity and the exemplary lives of its members.

As for Paul, however, he had already determined what ought to be done, what indeed would be done if he were present in the congregation. In fact, he pictures the solemn act of discipline as being performed: "Consider me, then, as if present among you, and with your cooperation, pronouncing in the name of Christ, the judgment of excommunication on this man and remanding him to Satan, that he may inflict upon him sufferings which will break the power of his sinful lusts, so that he may be led to repentance and recovery, and thus be saved at last at Christ's coming."

It is to be noted that Paul does not take the exercise of discipline out of the hands of the church. The government is democratic and the infliction of penalties is not entrusted to an officer or a priesthood.

Again it is to be noted that in the assembly, besides Paul's imagined presence, a third supreme Spirit presides and gives authority to execute the dread doom.

It is not to be supposed that this somewhat obscure incident in the history of the early church gives any sanction for the infliction of bodily punishment as an instrument of church discipline. Under the guidance of an inspired apostle and involving miraculous power, a sentence of bodily sickness or suffering seems to have been passed upon the guilty party. These factors are absent from all cases of church discipline in subsequent times.

Most important of all is it to observe that the suffering, whatever its nature or source, was intended to lead to repentance, so that it must ever be remembered that the supreme aim of all church discipline is the reformation of the offender.

2. THE SINFUL INDIFFERENCE   Ch. 5:6-8

As Paul continues to dwell upon the criminal carelessness of the Corinthians in their failure to punish the gross offender, he intimates another prime purpose of church discipline, namely, to protect the moral life of the church. "Your glorying is not good," writes the apostle. It is blind and stupid of you to be rejoicing in your teachers and in your spiritual attainments while you are tolerating such shameless sin.

"Know ye not that a little leaven leaveneth the whole lump?" This is a familiar figure of speech. A small amount of yeast soon affects the entire lump of dough. So the least complicity with evil, the countenancing of sin, the tolerating of impurity, affects the moral life of the whole church. It lowers moral standards and encourages other, if less flagrant, faults.

"Purge out the old leaven, that ye may be a new lump, even as ye are unleavened"; take out of your hearts all the evil dispositions and desires which belong to your former life and were natural to you before you knew Christ, that as a church you may be characterized by a new life, and may be in reality and experience what you might be as Christians and what, indeed, you are in the mind and purpose of God.

In enforcing this precept the apostle employs a beautiful and illuminating figure. On the eve of the first day of

the Passover feast the Israelites were compelled to remove
from their houses all leaven; and from the time when the
paschal lamb was sacrificed in the Temple no leavened
bread was allowed to appear on the table during all the
continuance of the feast.   Christ is our Paschal Lamb.
Life for us as followers of Christ is a holy feast.   If, therefore, we have accepted Christ, we should exclude from
our lives all sin, all the "old leaven" which characterized
us before we knew Christ, all "malice and wickedness";
and we should live lives of transparent sincerity and absolute truthfulness and reality.   "For our passover also hath
been sacrificed, even Christ: wherefore let us keep the
feast, not with old leaven, neither with the leaven of malice
and wickedness, but with the unleavened bread of sincerity and truth."

3. THE OBVIOUS SPHERE   Ch. 5:9-13

In a previous letter Paul had strenuously enjoined the
Corinthians against contaminating fellowship with fornicators.   This instruction had been misunderstood as for-
bidding all dealings with immoral persons, and had been
denounced as an impossible requirement.   It is probable
that this misinterpretation had been used as an excuse for
inaction in reference to the guilty members of the church.
Therefore Paul explains his meaning and insists that discipline must be administered.

"In a previous letter," he says in substance, "I warned
you not to associate with men like the one just mentioned;
but I did not mean that you are to have no relations in
the world at large with such men, or with greedy and
grasping men, or with idol worshipers; it would be wholly
impossible, as you suggest, to avoid all association with
such men; in that case you would have to leave the world
altogether.   What I meant to say, and I now repeat it, was
that if a professing Christian is guilty of such sins you
should withdraw from all fellowship with him.   Do not

even eat with such a person. I cannot undertake to regulate the outside world in such matters. I am content to keep the church without reproach, and that is equally your own duty. Our discipline cannot extend to those outside the church. These we leave to the judgment of God. But I have said enough. Excommunicate that wicked man."

It is evident that Paul here gives no encouragement to needless association and intimacies with men of the world. In his next epistle he deals specifically with the peril of being "unequally yoked with unbelievers."

It is further evident that the purpose of church discipline is not only the reformation of the offender, and the preservation of the moral purity of the church, but in the third place it is the defense of the good name and fame of the church. Every effort must be made to show the world that the church of Christ will not tolerate moral evil within its bounds. Possibly the time has come now for the church to consider the discipline, not only of men guilty of the gross sins with which this section of the epistle especially deals but also of those who are "greedy of gain," and "guilty of extortion," and "abusive in their language." Such action might cause some consternation in our complacent modern church, but it might bring a stirring, surprising, awakening message to an unbelieving world.

C. LAWSUITS   Ch. 6:1-11

1 Dare any of you, having a matter against his neighbor, go to law before the unrighteous, and not before the saints? 2 Or know ye not that the saints shall judge the world? and if the world is judged by you, are ye unworthy to judge the smallest matters? 3 Know ye not that we shall judge angels? how much more, things that pertain to this life? 4 If then ye have to judge things pertaining to this life, do ye set them to judge who are of no account in the church? 5 I say this *to move you to shame. What, cannot there be* found *among you one wise man who shall be able to decide between his brethren, 6 but brother goeth to law with*

*brother, and that before unbelievers? 7 Nay, already it is
altogether a defect in you, that ye have lawsuits one with
another. Why not rather take wrong? why not rather be
defrauded? 8 Nay, but ye yourselves do wrong, and defraud, and that your brethren. 9 Or know ye not that the
unrighteous shall not inherit the kingdom of God? Be not
deceived: neither fornicators, nor idolators, nor adulterers,
nor effeminate, nor abusers of themselves with men, 10 nor
thieves, nor covetous, nor drunkards, nor revilers, nor extortioners, shall inherit the kingdom of God. 11 And such
were some of you: but ye were washed, but ye were sanctified, but ye were justified in the name of the Lord Jesus
Christ, and in the Spirit of our God.*

Paul has just stated the necessity on the part of the
church of judging and condemning an offending member.
Quite naturally he turns to consider a growing practice
among the Corinthian Christians of appearing as contestants in the courts of law. This practice had become so
frequent as to constitute a scandal.

It is easy to understand how these Greeks, fond of ora-
tory, fond of debate, fond of the excitement of a contest,
had a natural liking for litigation. However, Paul indicates that the litigators were often impelled by less worthy
motives. The lawsuits were employed as means of defrauding and injuring their fellow Christians. Therefore
the apostle states two principles: first, that it is shameful
for Christians to be continually contending before pagan
judges (vs. 1-6), and second, that lawsuits between Christians indicate a lack of righteousness and love (vs. 8-11).

"Dare any of you, having a matter against his neighbor,
go to law before the unrighteous, and not before the
saints?" The shame of referring these matters to heathen
judges is made apparent by two reasons: the high calling
and destiny of Christians, and the low estimate in which
such judges are held by the church.

"Know ye not that the saints shall judge the world? . . .
Know ye not that we shall judge angels?" It is idle to

speculate as to the exact conditions to which the apostle refers, or as to the nature of that future state in which Christians are to be given such dignity and power. Paul has a startling way of introducing, thus casually, truths so full of mystery and meaning. These references afford most imperfect glimpses of the coming age of glory. However, they indicate that Christians are never to become angels, but are to be superior to angels; that Christians are to share with Christ rule over a renewed world; and that, therefore, they should be competent now to settle among themselves trivial disputes, and questions relating to this present life.

It is, indeed, shameful for such persons to refer their controversies to heathen judges who have no such high destiny and who even now have no standing in the estimate of the church. "Surely there must be some one in your company of Christians," concludes the apostle, "who is capable of deciding such disputes; you do not need to go to heathen courts." Differences between Christians should be settled by arbitration.

Paul does not mean that a Christian is never to seek for justice in the civil courts and is under no conditions to demand the protection of law. "The powers that be are ordained of God"; and the people of God have a perfect right to accept all the benefits which stable government and just laws confer.

However, Paul is stating a rule. Quarrels between Christians and lawsuits in the public courts are occasions for scandal, and should be avoided. In fact, the apostle proceeds to say that such lawsuits are sinful. "Nay, already it is altogether a defect in you, that ye have lawsuits one with another." Indeed, it is more than a defect. The word may be translated "a defeat." The contestants are beaten before they enter court. The very fact that disputes have arisen and reached such a point is an evidence of moral defeat.

Thus the cause and the evil of these lawsuits is traced

to the purpose of injuring and defrauding fellow Christians, or to the bitter resentment and desire for revenge on the part of those who have been wronged. Such litigation is indeed sinful. Rather than be overcome by these faults it would be better to avoid such lawsuits altogether. For Paul warns his readers that "the unrighteous shall not inherit the kingdom of God."

Those who wrong their fellow Christians are worthy to be classed with the unclean and covetous and wicked persons who are excluded from that Kingdom. In their guilty contentions these Corinthians were manifesting the very spirit of the world from which they had been delivered. Therefore, they should cease from their strifes and conduct themselves as men who have been washed clean from every stain, who have been set apart as holy, who have been pronounced just, in the name of the Lord Jesus Christ and through the Spirit of our God.

D. IMPURITY Ch. 6:12-20

12 All things are lawful for me; but not all things are expedient. All things are lawful for me; but I will not be brought under the power of any. 13 Meats for the belly, and the belly for meats: but God shall bring to nought both it and them. But the body is not for fornication, but for the Lord; and the Lord for the body: 14 and God both raised the Lord, and will raise up us through his power. 15 Know ye not that your bodies are members of Christ? shall I then take away the members of Christ, and make them members of a harlot? God forbid. 16 Or know ye not that he that is joined to a harlot is one body? for, The twain, saith he, shall become one flesh. 17 But he that is joined unto the Lord is one spirit. 18 Flee fornication. Every sin that a man doeth is without the body; but he that committeth fornication sinneth against his own body. 19 Or know ye not that your body is a temple of the Holy Spirit which is in you, which ye have from God? and ye are not your own; 20 for ye were bought with a price: glorify God therefore in your body.

The third moral question which Paul discusses is that of impurity. He had shown that the lawsuits which the Corinthian Christians were employing to defraud and injure one another were sinful, and were manifesting the unrighteous spirit which was expressed in the heathen vices from which Christians had been redeemed. He now finds it necessary to refer to the most prevalent of these vices, namely, that of impurity.

"To live as a Corinthian" was in Paul's day a proverbial description of a life of immorality and unchastity. The practice of impurity formed a feature of idolatrous worship. It is not altogether surprising, therefore, that even some Christians at Corinth had concluded that the eating of meats offered to idols and fornication were both matters of moral indifference.

Paul had taught the doctrine of Christian liberty. He had insisted that a Christian could observe or not observe the holy days of the ancient Hebrews, and that he could eat or refuse to eat food which had been used in idol worship. These were questions of conscience, as to which Christians might differ, and he discusses them at length in the eighth and ninth and tenth chapters of this epistle.

This principle of Christian liberty had evidently been advanced in excuse for the practice of impurity. Paul maintains the principle but makes certain exceptions, and then denies its application to a practice which was not a matter of moral indifference but a heinous sin.

His first exception states that while all things which are morally indifferent may be lawful for a Christian, yet not all such things may be advantageous: "All things are lawful for me; but not all things are expedient." Even if impurity had not been forbidden specifically by the law of God, it could be shown to be injurious.

In the second place, while a Christian may indulge in all things morally indifferent, yet the very indulgence may lead to spiritual slavery: "All things are lawful for me; but I will not be brought under the power of any." Even a habit which could not be called immoral may completely master a man. He is uneasy and distressed until he has satisfied the craving he has created. Even if impurity were not so obviously immoral, it is incomparably enslaving and cannot be defended on the ground of Christian liberty. "The reasonable use of my liberty cannot go to the length of involving my own loss of it."

With these two restrictions, the question of eating various kinds of food is a matter of moral indifference; but impurity is a very different matter. It is a direct violation of specific divine law, and is not merely an innocent indulgence of a natural appetite.

However, Paul does not discountenance this sin on the sole ground that it is a breach of the Seventh Commandment, which applies to every man, but on the even higher ground of the relation in which the believer stands to Christ his Lord.

In the case of food, it is intended for the stomach and the stomach is adapted to the digestion of food. Neither can attain a higher object, neither belongs to a higher sphere, and both are designed for our present needs and mode of life. The whole body, however, the instrument of our immortal souls, was not intended for impurity—far from it—but "for the Lord; and the Lord for the body"; and both are forever.

The body is "for the Lord." This is its design and end. He finds in it his needed instrument. He owns it; he dwells in it. He has redeemed it. Someday he will transfigure it with glory.

"The Lord is for the body." To it he must give directions for the proper use of all its impulses and powers. Without him it can never attain its true dignity and its immortal destiny.

This relationship which our bodies sustain to Christ is eternal. "God both raised the Lord, and will raise up us through his power." In the fifteenth chapter of this epistle Paul dwells at length upon this theme. How the identity of the present body is to be maintained, or in what it is to consist, Paul does not explain; but that the body does have such an immortal and glorious destiny Paul affirms on the assured ground of the resurrection of Christ.

The bodies of Christians therefore belong to Christ. They are like members of his own body. Can these members then be surrendered to the service of impurity? Unhallowed and impure unions are nonetheless real in their nature and influence, as real as was the union of our first parents in Eden, but no more real than the spiritual union between the believer and Christ. Impurity is, therefore, disloyalty and treason against Christ.

Flee from this sin, writes the apostle. Not only fight against it, but avoid its occasion, for this, above all sins, defiles the body. It is preeminently the sin against the body. The body of the Christian is sacred to God. One has no right to defile it. Impurity often formed a part of the worship in the heathen temples. On the contrary, the bodies of Christians should be kept pure as temples of God's Spirit.

Moreover, Christians are not their own. They have been purchased by the precious blood of Christ. Believers, therefore, by the purity and holiness of their lives, should honor him to whom they belong. The whole passage indicates the unique teaching of Christianity in reference to the dignity and sanctity of the human body. Christian liberty is not to be interpreted as license to indulge in fleshly sins, nor yet is the highest spiritual attainment to be regarded as an excuse for the neglect or abuse of the body, which is to be regarded as a holy instrument of Christ, as a sacred temple for the indwelling of the Spirit of God.

The last statement is an illustration of the ability of Paul to set forth the most beautiful truths like sparkling gems against the dark foil of prevalent impurity and sin, and further to employ the most sublime realities as motives for the most elemental moral virtues. Thus in deal-

ing with these three questions of discipline and litigation
and impurity, while treating of matters most delicate and
difficult and distasteful, he gives in the first instance the
touching exhortation: "Our passover also hath been sacrificed, even Christ: wherefore let us keep the feast . . .
with the unleavened bread of sincerity and truth." In rebuking abuse of lawsuits, he reminds us that Christians
are yet to "judge the world," and to "judge angels." In
warning against impurity he makes the superb affirmation
that our bodies are temples "of the Holy Spirit."

E. MARRIAGE   Ch. 7

A number of problems had been presented to Paul by
the Corinthians in a letter of inquiry. Among these were
questions relative to marriage. Having just treated the
subject of social purity, the apostle naturally turns next
to answer these questions, for he regarded the institution
of marriage as one of the safeguards by which such purity
is preserved.

It is to be noted, however, that he does not treat marriage as a matter of morality but of expediency. He never
insists that it is right or wrong but that it is a question
to be determined by conditions and temperament. He
has discussed, as moral issues, the questions involved in
church discipline, in litigation, and in personal purity, but
he now passes to consider two questions which he treats
as matters of moral indifference, namely, marriage and
the eating of meats offered to idols. Thus while keeping
it closely linked to the preceding section, Paul here begins
a distinct division of his epistle.

For the teaching here given in reference to marriage
Paul has been severely criticized. It is very easy to misunderstand his statements. Two or three facts should be
borne in mind. First, he is here answering specific questions as to the exact content of which we are not informed.
Were he discussing the entire subject of marriage in all its

aspects, his treatment would have been far different. The larger aspects and the spiritual import of marriage are presented in other portions of his epistles.

Then again, the manner and method of his discussion and the special arguments employed could be fully understood only in the light of the erroneous opinions existing in the church at Corinth, and as to these, we are not fully informed. It seems certain, at least, that some Christians regarded marriage as an absolute duty. Others considered the marriage state as an inferior moral condition, a weak concession to the flesh. Still others held that by accepting Christ all existing social relationships, including marriage, were dissolved.

In the third place it should be noted that Paul writes with reference to certain conditions which were purely local and temporary. To apply his every injunction literally and to Christians in all ages would be misleading. The underlying principles by which he is guided are changeless. Usually it is not very difficult to distinguish between the immediate application to changing conditions and the abiding truth on which his instruction rests. When fairly interpreted, his teaching here relative to marriage appears peculiarly sane and wise and embodies principles which are of present and permanent value.

While his treatment is not exhaustive, it deals with the four following phases of the subject: marriage and celibacy (vs. 1-9); marriage and divorce (vs. 10-24); marriage and Christian service (vs. 25-38); marriage "in the Lord" (vs. 39-40).

1. FORMING THE TIE, OR MARRIAGE AND CELIBACY   Ch. 7:1-9

1 Now concerning the things whereof ye wrote: It is good for a man not to touch a woman. 2 But, because of fornications, let each man have his own wife, and let each woman have her own husband. 3 Let the husband render unto the wife her due: and likewise also the wife unto the husband. 4 The wife hath not power over her own body, but the husband: and likewise also the husband hath not power over his own body, but the wife. 5 Defraud ye not one the other, except it be by consent for a season, that ye may give yourselves unto prayer, and may be together again, that Satan tempt you not because of your incontinency. 6 But this I say by way of concession, not of commandment. 7 Yet I would that all men were even as I myself. Howbeit each man hath his own gift from God, one after this manner, and another after that.

8 But I say to the unmarried and to widows, It is good for them if they abide even as I. 9 But if they have not continency, let them marry: for it is better to marry than to burn.

Paul has been misinterpreted as a narrow ascetic who despised women and discouraged marriage. On the contrary, he advised marriage as the rule for all Christians, and regarded celibacy as embodying no superior moral virtue. In reading this entire chapter and interpreting all that Paul has to say on the subject, this fundamental truth should be kept in mind.

While marriage is to be the rule, the apostle insists that celibacy is an honorable estate. "It is good for a man not to touch a woman." There is no special virtue in marrying. Paul is here defending celibacy against those who regard it as wrong and unchristian. Indeed, celibacy has certain advantages which Paul relates in a later paragraph (vs. 25-38). However, marriage should be the rule. It must be true marriage, the abiding union of one man and one woman: "Let each man have his own wife, and let each woman have her own husband." Such an institution aids in preserving the moral purity on which organized society must rest. Lax views of marriage strike at the life of the family and threaten the continuance of the social order. Those teachers at Corinth who so exalted celibacy as to discountenance marriage needed to be corrected and rebuked. Marriage was ordained of God in Eden and sanctified by the gracious presence of Christ and by his miraculous gift in Cana of Galilee, and upon it as a Christian institution Paul places his unqualified seal and approval.

There was, however, another strange error held by most Corinthian Christians. They supposed that marriage, in contrast with celibacy, was such an inferior condition that it would be meritorious for married Christians to cease to live in marriage relations. This error Paul rebukes. Such a practice would involve needless temptation. Husbands and wives should fulfill their mutual obligations. If for a time they refrain, it must not be as a matter of merit but by mutual consent and for some wise reason, such as for special seasons of prayer.

Paul declares that in stating marriage to be the rule of Christians he is saying this "by way of concession, not of commandment." Some have falsely interpreted him as meaning that he was not writing under divine direction. What he really means is that his inspired advice to marry is not to be construed as a command, but as a matter of permission. Each person is free to act according to circumstances and disposition.

The apostle, however, declares his own preference for an unmarried life in case that life is free from restlessness and dissatisfaction. While he regards celibacy as excellent, he declares the capacity for celibacy to be a special gift. Those who do not possess this gift should marry. The teaching of the apostle is obviously sane and reasonable. It is absurd to insist that all persons should marry. Some may be happier and may fulfill their course of life with more of comfort and satisfaction if they remain unmarried. The usual rule, however, is marriage; the exception is a case like that of Paul. It is folly for one to take a vow of celibacy unless he possesses the special capacity and gift.

2. Loosing the Tie, or Marriage and Divorce
Ch. 7:10-24

10 But unto the married I give charge, yea not I, but the Lord, That the wife depart not from her husband 11 (but should she depart, let her remain unmarried, or else be reconciled to her husband); and that the husband leave not his wife. 12 But to the rest say I, not the Lord: If any brother hath an unbelieving wife, and she is content to dwell with him, let him not leave her. 13 And the woman that hath an unbelieving husband, and he is content to dwell with her, let her not leave her husband. 14 For the unbelieving husband is sanctified in the wife, and the unbelieving wife is sanctified in the brother: else were your children unclean; but now are they holy. 15 Yet if the unbelieving departeth, let him depart: the brother or the sister is not under bondage in such cases: but God hath called us in peace. 16 For how knowest thou, O wife, whether thou shalt save thy husband? or how knowest thou, O husband, whether thou shalt save thy wife? 17 Only, as the Lord hath distributed to each man, as God hath called each, so let him walk. And so ordain I in all the churches. 18 Was any man called being circumcised? let him not become uncircumcised. Hath any been called in uncircumcision? let him not be circumcised. 19 Circumcision is nothing, and uncircumcision is nothing; but the keeping of the commandments of God. 20 Let each man abide in that calling wherein he was called. 21 Wast thou called being a bondservant? care not for it: nay, even if thou canst become free, use it rather. 22 For he that was called in the Lord being a bondservant, is the Lord's freedman: likewise he that was called being free, is Christ's bondservant. 23 Ye were bought with a price; become not bondservants of men. 24 Brethren, let each man, wherein he was called, therein abide with God.

It has been observed that there were those at Corinth who believed that the acceptance of Christ involved the severance of all social ties, including those of marriage. Certain Christians, therefore, deemed it necessary to separate from their Christian partners and to live lives of celibacy. Others felt that if a husband or wife became a Christian, he or she should seek divorce from an unbelieving spouse.

Paul states and illustrates the rule applying to both classes and to all social relations and conditions: "Let each man abide in that calling wherein he was called." Social ties and relationships are not to be disturbed or severed but to be glorified by the acceptance of Christ as Lord.

As to the first class, Paul reminds them of the explicit command of Christ which forbids divorce save on the one ground of unfaithfulness: "But unto the married I give charge, yea not I, but the Lord, That the wife depart not from her husband . . . and that the husband leave not his wife." Paul adds, however, that if there is a separation, remarriage to other parties is impossible. Christians who separate must remain unmarried or else be reconciled to each other.

The course to be followed in the case of those involved in mixed marriages, "the rest," is more difficult to determine (vs. 12-16). When one partner has become a Christian subsequent to marriage, is not this change of faith sufficient ground for divorce? Shall a Christian husband or wife be compelled to live with a heathen? Christ left no explicit answer to his question, but Paul under divine inspiration gives one. He does not here disclaim inspiration; he rather invests his reply with the very same authority as that of Christ's previous command. He means that he has no word of the Master to quote but he has specific directions to give: "But to the rest say I, not the Lord."

His statement is to the effect that becoming a Christian is no ground for divorce, nor is the unbelief of a partner in marriage. "Let each man abide in that calling wherein he was called" is the injunction of the apostle. If a separation does take place, it must be due to the action of the unbelieving partner. If the unbeliever is content to dwell with the Christian, the believer is not to seek a separation. The unbelieving partner and the children of such a union are brought under the sanctifying influence of a Christian life. Paul does not here sanction the marriage of a Christian to an unbeliever. This he discourages. (II Cor. 6:14.) He does teach, however, that the acceptance of Christ by either a husband or a wife brings into the family circle a holy atmosphere and the possibilities of a Christian home.

However, if an unbelieving partner insists upon a separation, the believer must acquiesce. To insist upon a continuance of the marriage relation would only lead to strife. The Christian "is not under bondage in such cases." A separation is advisable. "God hath called us in peace." It is, of course, possible that a continuance of the union might result in the conversion of the unbelieving husband or wife, but this result is by no means certain. The more evident advantages of separation in such cases outweigh this remote contingency.

It is to be noted that nothing is said here as to the right of remarriage. As Paul has just declared remarriage to be impossible for Christians who separate, such a prohibition would naturally be implied in the case of a separation between a Christian and an unbeliever, in case nothing is stated to the contrary. Furthermore, it is most improbable that Paul would contradict the explicit command of Christ who allowed divorce and remarriage only on the ground of unfaithfulness. If an unbelieving husband or wife who has caused such a separation subsequently marries, then, according to the very teaching of our Lord, the deserted party would be absolutely free to contract a new marriage, with a believer.

While such separations as Paul has described may be allowed, and even necessary, the apostle by no means encourages them. The rule should be that the marriage relationship should not be lightly broken. One should fulfill all the duties of that relationship in which he has been providentially placed and in which the call to be a Christian found him: "As the Lord hath distributed to each man, as God hath called each, so let him walk."

Paul applies this principle to the two chief political and social distinctions of the day. If a Jew became a Christian, he was to be content to be a Christian Jew. For Christians, national distinctions are of no great importance, but obedience to God is everything. Christianity does not design to break down national and social distinctions. If a slave became a Christian, his inferior position was not to cause him anxiety; he was to use his very servitude in a Christian way and not seek to become free on the ground that he had become a Christian. In Christ social distinctions disappear in a higher unity. The Christian slave is Christ's freeman, and the Christian freeman is Christ's slave. We have been bought with a great price and belong to one Master. We must not become slaves of men, yielding to their views and seeking to change the condition in which the call of Christ found us. In respect to his social or political state, each one should abide in relationship with God.

3. UNMARRIED WOMEN, OR MARRIAGE AND CHRISTIAN SERVICE   Ch. 7:25-38

25 Now concerning virgins I have no commandment of the Lord: but I give my judgment, as one that hath obtained mercy of the Lord to be trustworthy. 26 I think therefore that this is good by reason of the distress that is upon us, namely, that it is good for a man to be as he is. 27 Art thou bound unto a wife? seek not to be loosed. Art thou loosed from a wife? seek not a wife. 28 But shouldest thou marry, thou hast not sinned; and if a virgin marry, she hath not sinned. Yet such shall have tribulation in the flesh: and I would spare you. 29 But this I say, brethren, the time is shortened, that henceforth both those that have wives may be as though they had none; 30 and those that weep, as though they wept not; and those that

*rejoice, as though they rejoiced not; and those that buy, as
though they possessed not; 31 and those that use the
world, as not using it to the full: for the fashion of this
world passeth away. 32 But I would have you to be free
from cares. He that is unmarried is careful for the things
of the Lord, how he may please the Lord: 33 but he that
is married is careful for the things of the world, how he
may please his wife, 34 and is divided.* So also the woman
*that is unmarried and the virgin is careful for the things
of the Lord, that she may be holy both in body and in
spirit: but she that is married is careful for the things of
the world, how she may please her husband. 35 And this
I say for your own profit; not that I may cast a snare upon
you, but for that which is seemly, and that ye may attend
upon the Lord without distraction. 36 But if any man
thinketh that he behaveth himself unseemly toward his
virgin* daughter, *if she be past the flower of her age, and if
need so requireth, let him do what he will; he sinneth not;
let them marry. 37 But he that standeth stedfast in his
heart, having no necessity, but hath power as touching his
own will, and hath determined this in his own heart, to
keep his own virgin* daughter, *shall do well. 38 So then
both he that giveth his own virgin* daughter *in marriage
doeth well; and he that giveth her not in marriage shall do
better.*

Paul had been asked advice as to the duty of parents in
reference to their unmarried daughters. Ought they to
give them in marriage or should they withhold their consent? As to this he declares he has "no commandment of
the Lord." He means not only that Christ gave no teaching in this matter, but that his reply is not to be in the
form of a rule or a requirement but of advice in which
parents may or may not concur, as circumstances may
determine. Paul here is not disclaiming inspiration but
says that he is one who rightly can be trusted.

His reply is in substance to the effect that amid present
hardships and difficulties it may be wiser for a person to
remain unmarried. Distress may be avoided and Christian

service less hampered. However, it is not a matter of right
and wrong but of expediency and personal choice.

There are thus three elements in Paul's reply. First,
"by reason of the distress that is upon us," it may be well
to remain unmarried, or if married, one should accept
patiently the responsibilities of such a life. The present
age will soon end. The suspense awaiting the coming of
Christ will cease. The present sufferings of Christians
may be those predicted immediately to precede the Lord's
return. Therefore, marriage and other human relations
should not occupy our thoughts too completely or cause
us undue anxiety. Parents should not suppose that the
marriage of their daughters is the most important thing in
the world.

Paul's words are not to be pressed too far. He did not
affirm that Christ would come immediately, or that Christians should disregard the normal duties and sacred relationships of life. This would be contrary to the remainder
of this chapter and to other sections of this epistle. He
wishes, however, that his readers may view things in their
right proportions and, since the present order of the world
is not the permanent order, that they should not be concerned too seriously with conditions and relations which
will soon pass away. He wished them to "use the world"
but not to be absorbed in it, "for the fashion of this world
passeth away."   (Vs. 26-31.)

In the second place, Paul declares that in the times of
distress which were upon the church there were advantages
in celibacy. One not married would be far more free to
render various forms of Christian service, and possibly
would be less tempted and perplexed by worldly distrac-
tions. That one might be "free from cares" is declared to
be the end he aims to secure by his advice. He desires to
further the advantage of his readers. He does not wish
to abridge their liberty, but to help them to do what is
becoming, that they may serve the Lord without distraction.

In the third place, Paul emphasizes the fact that the attitude and action of a parent in reference to a daughter's marriage is purely a matter of expediency and of circumstances. If any father thinks he is acting unfairly toward his unmarried daughter, particularly if she has passed the bloom of youth, and if there is a real necessity in the case, by all means let him give her in marriage. In so doing he commits no fault. If, on the contrary, he refuses to give his daughter in marriage, it must be on such conditions as Paul proceeds to lay down: He must have a definite conviction as to the wisdom of his course. There must be no opposing necessity such as an existing engagement to marry or other determining circumstance. He must possess the legal and moral right to exercise his restraint; such rights did not always exist under Roman law, and according to the social system of Paul's day. Then again, his decision must have been reached deliberately and independently.

If all these conditions are fulfilled, it may be better in days of distress and hardship to follow this course. Nevertheless, "he that giveth his own virgin daughter in marriage doeth well." There is nothing wrong in his action. However, there may be circumstances and conditions when by continuing an unmarried life the service of Christ and growth in Christian character may be more definite and free.

4. WIDOWS, OR MARRIAGE IN THE LORD
Ch. 7:39-40

39 A wife is bound for so long time as her husband liveth; but if the husband be dead, she is free to be married to whom she will; only in the Lord. 40 But she is happier if she abide as she is, after my judgment: and I think that I also have the Spirit of God.

While the case of widows has been covered in a measure by Paul's previous instruction, he adds a more definite word as he concludes his reply to the questions which had been proposed to him relative to marriage. He declares that death breaks the marriage bond, so that after the death of her husband a wife "is free to be married to whom she will." Paul does not intimate that there is anything wrong or unseemly or unchristian in second marriages. In fact, in another connection he urges young widows to marry: "I desire therefore that the younger widows marry, bear children, rule the household, give no occasion to the adversary for reviling" (I Tim. 5:14). Nevertheless, in this connection where Paul has been referring to the difficult times which were upon the church, he does add in reference to a widow that while she is free to remarry, it is his opinion that "she is happier if she abide as she is." It is to be noted, however, that Paul is not only writing this chapter in view of the unusual circumstances of distress and persecution to which Christians were submitted, but he has always insisted that the question of marriage is one of expediency, the wisdom of which must be determined in every case by specific circumstances and conditions.

It is evident, however, that Paul is allowing remarriage not in the case of divorce, but only in the case of the death of a husband. As he states, "A wife is bound for so long time as her husband liveth."

The particular emphasis, however, which Paul lays on this instruction relative to the marriage of widows is found in the words "only in the Lord." It is very evident that Paul does not encourage Christians to marry unbelievers. When he puts this particular restraint upon the marriage of widows, he means to say, however, that not only should the marriage be with a believer but also it should be undertaken with Christian motives and such as could receive the sanction of Christ.

Paul concludes this long chapter of advice with a claim which should be kept in mind by many who feel that in certain earlier verses he has disclaimed inspiration: "And

I think [whatever others may say of me] that I also have [an inspiration of] the Spirit of God."

The chapter cannot be read lightly. It demands careful study lest it may be misunderstood. In it there may be many references to conditions which are purely temporary, but all Christians would do well to ponder seriously the underlying principles which Paul here proclaims. They are applicable to many of the most serious problems of present-day life. They may erect standards too high for the social customs of the day, but no higher than those which should be observed by the followers of Christ. His teaching here is not to be regarded as the passing opinions of an ancient writer. The advice which this chapter sets forth came from one who was conscious that its source was not mere unaided human opinion and that it had the sanction of the Spirit of God.

F. THE USE OF MEAT SACRIFICED TO IDOLS   Chs. 8:1 to 11:1

Some things are approved by all men as right; others are as universally condemned as wrong. There is, however, a third group of acts and practices as to the moral quality of which opinions differ. They are forbidden by the conscience of one man, and by the conscience of another equally good they are allowed.

Such in the church at Corinth was the question of eating meat which previously had been offered in sacrifice to heathen gods. Many Christians regarded idolatry as a mere superstition and knew that the meat which had been offered in heathen worship had contracted no moral quality. In the mind of others, however, to partake of food which had been used in idol temples involved complicity with idolatry and was regarded as morally wrong.

Such are the questions of conscience which confront Christians today: to some they seem to be matters of moral indifference; to others they involve serious questions of right and wrong. Such are the problems relating to the forms of Sabbath observance, to social amusements, to personal expenditures, and to indulgences.

The question was very serious for the Christians at Corinth. Idolatrous practices were related to almost every family and social and political custom of the times. Meats which had been sacrificed in the temple were used at all social festivities; they were exposed for sale in the regular markets and were placed upon the table before invited guests and might appear in one's own home. It was, therefore, a very difficult and delicate problem which had been referred to the apostle by his friends at Corinth.

Paul might have appealed to the decision of the Council at Jerusalem, which had prohibited the use of meats sacrificed to idols. This decision, however, seems to have been local and temporary in its application. Furthermore, the use of any explicit rule was contrary to Paul's method in dealing with the problems of the Corinthian church. Paul set forth principles which he taught his readers to apply to their various problems. It is this method which makes his letter of such abiding value. The very principles which he lays down in reference to the eating of meat which had been offered to idols apply at the present day to all questions of conscience, and offer valuable guidance in solving some of our most pressing and practical problems.

In a previous chapter, in reference to matters of moral indifference, Paul had stated that even in a matter of Christian liberty he would not allow himself to be enslaved by a habit which in itself might be innocent: "All things are lawful for me; but I will not be brought under the power of any" (I Cor. 6:12).

Furthermore, in his epistle to the Romans (chs. 14:1 to 15:13), Paul gives instructions relative to these same problems. However, his most exhaustive treatment of these questions is found in the three chapters of this epistle which immediately follow. The principles set forth may possibly be outlined in five passages:

Indulgence may imperil the weak; therefore liberty must be regulated by love.   (Ch. 8.)

Indulgence may hinder Christian work; therefore be all things to all men. (Ch. 9.)

Indulgence may endanger the soul; therefore take heed lest you fall. (Ch. 10:1-13.)

Indulgence may identify with the world; therefore do not provoke Christ to jealousy. (Ch. 10:14-22.)

Consider what is expedient and edifies; and do all to the glory of God. (Chs. 10:23 to 11:1.)

1. THE PROBLEM   Ch. 8

1 Now concerning things sacrificed to idols: We know that we all have knowledge. Knowledge puffeth up, but love edifieth. 2 If any man thinketh that he knoweth anything, he knoweth not yet as he ought to know; 3 but if any man loveth God, the same is known by him. 4 Concerning therefore the eating of things sacrificed to idols, we know that no idol is anything in the world, and that there is no God but one. 5 For though there be that are called gods, whether in heaven or on earth; as there are gods many, and lords many; 6 yet to us there is one God, the Father, of whom are all things, and we unto him; and one Lord, Jesus Christ, through whom are all things, and we through him. 7 Howbeit there is not in all men that knowledge: but some, being used until now to the idol, eat as of a thing sacrificed to an idol; and their conscience being weak is defiled. 8 But food will not commend us to God: neither, if we eat not, are we the worse; nor, if we eat, are we the better. 9 But take heed lest by any means this liberty of yours become a stumblingblock to the weak. 10 For if a man see thee who hast knowledge sitting at meat in an idol's temple, will not his conscience, if he is weak, be emboldened to eat things sacrificed to idols? 11 For through thy knowledge he that is weak perisheth, the brother for whose sake Christ died. 12 And thus, sinning against the brethren, and wounding their conscience when it is weak, ye sin against Christ. 13 Wherefore, if meat causeth my brother to stumble, I will eat no flesh for evermore, that I cause not my brother to stumble.

In dealing with questions of moral indifference, as to which the answers of Christians equally good do not agree, Paul in theory defends Christian freedom but in practice he imposes rather severe restrictions. Thus in this chapter, after stating clearly the problem concerning the use of meat which had been offered in sacrifice to idols, he states the first great principle, that liberty must be limited by love. He insists that difficult and delicate questions involved cannot be settled from the standpoint of knowledge and its rights, but must be determined by love and its obligations.

In regard to the question of eating the meat of animals killed in idolatrous sacrifice, Paul declares that enlightened Christians know that such meat can have no defiling effect. He states, however, that in the Christian life, love and not knowledge is the safest guide. Knowledge puffs up, but love builds up. The man who thinks that he knows anything perfectly does not yet possess one of the essential elements of true knowledge, and one who determines to act solely in accordance with what is theoretically allowable has not yet learned the Christian way of life. But if anyone loves God, that man is truly known by God and has entered into a blessed and divine fellowship. As to "the eating of things sacrificed to idols," Paul declares that Christians understand that "no idol is anything in the world." It is a mere creation of the imagination, a mere matter of superstition. A Christian knows that "there is no God but one." According to the religions of the heathen there are numerous so-called divinities, yet in the Christian belief there is only one God. He is the Source and the End of all things. He is the Creator of all things and Christians are for his service and glory. There is but one Lord, Jesus Christ; through him all things were created, and through him we Christians have been brought into the service of God.

However, not all men share this knowledge. Some Christians whose faith is imperfect and who have been brought up to think of heathen deities as possessing actual power cannot rid themselves of the idea that meat which has been used in heathen sacrifice is defiled and ought not to be eaten by a Christian. We know that our acceptance with God does not depend upon such matters. "The question of eating such food or not eating it, is itself morally indifferent; but while one is thus free to follow either course, he must consider how his action in so doing will affect others, and must regulate his own liberty by regard for their good." He must beware lest any action of his prove to be a stumbling block in the way of those whose consciences are less enlightened.

Suppose, for instance, that a person who is thus weak in the faith should see a fellow Christian who lacks his scruples partaking of an idolatrous feast. Would he not be encouraged to do what his conscience forbids? Would he thus not be emboldened to do what he regards as wrong? Would not one's boasted knowledge and his selfish use of liberty thus lead to the destruction of a brother for whose sake Christ died? Thus it is that the use of liberty, in itself allowable, may be a means of moral destruction to the weak Christian. To act with such reckless disregard for the weakness and ignorance of others is to do them a great moral injury and is to violate the law of Christ.

Therefore, Paul concludes that if the use of such food as has been offered to idols might cause his Christian brother to stumble, he would be willing, as long as he should live, to partake of no meat, lest he might cause another to offend.

When Paul speaks of a weak brother, he does not mean one who might easily be influenced to do wrong, but one who is weak in faith, who is overscrupulous, who does not understand the meaning of Christian liberty, and who does not see that the eating of food which has been offered in the worship of false gods is a matter of moral indifference.

From all that Paul has said, it is evident that conscience must always be obeyed. Its demands may be absurd but they cannot be disregarded. It is our duty to enlighten our consciences; we must never violate them. In questions of right and wrong, as to which Christians do not agree, foolish scruples sometimes may be removed by considering the counsel and example of others. However, one must not follow this example or advice until conscience approves.

On the other hand, we must never persuade another to act contrary to conscience; nor should we by our example knowingly embolden others so to act.

We must be willing even to refrain from what we regard as innocent if we believe that our example might lead others to do what they regard as wrong. We must not so refrain, however, if for any reason conscience forbids us to refrain. If, however, the matter is to us one of moral indifference, then love must determine our course. "To some extent we must be regulated in our conduct by the narrow-mindedness, the scruples, the prejudices, the weakness of others." One must endeavor "to keep step with the Christian community of which he forms a part."

Thus Paul sets forth this first great principle in reference to questions of conscience: Indulgence may imperil the weak; therefore liberty must be regulated by love.

2. THE EXAMPLE OF PAUL   Ch. 9

For matters of moral indifference where the opinions of Christians do not agree, Paul has laid down a first great principle that liberty must be regulated by love, and he has declared his willingness to abide by that principle so that if eating meat offered to idols might cause his brother to stumble, he would refrain from eating meat as long as he lived.

In stating the second principle, which should determine the course of Christians in such matters of conscience, Paul also offers himself as an example. He cites his own well-known practice at Corinth. In that city he had refused to accept any salary for his work in the church lest his motives might have been misinterpreted and his influence might have been injured. His course in other cities had been quite different. There he had gladly received remuneration for his work, at least support in his spiritual labor. In Corinth he followed one course, in other places a differing course, for the sake of the work in which he was engaged. In this he was an example of the important principle which is discussed in this ninth chapter of the epistle: Indulgence may hinder Christian work; therefore be "all things to all men."

It should be noted that Paul is still discussing the question of the use of meat which had been offered in idol worship. The principle which he illustrates by his renouncing of financial support at Corinth was intended to apply first of all to this question which had been proposed to him by the Corinthian church. Just as he has been willing to sacrifice his salary for the sake of the gospel, so these Christians must be willing to refrain from the use of such meat, should their partaking of it in any case lessen their influence with their fellow Christians.

It is for us who read this epistle today to make similar practical applications to questions of conscience by which we are continually confronted. We should be willing to sacrifice much that may seem innocent to us in case our indulgence might in any wise endanger our work for Christ.

a. Sacrifice for the Gospel's Sake   Ch. 9:1-18

1 Am I not free? am I not an apostle? have I not seen Jesus our Lord? are not ye my work in the Lord? 2 If to others I am not an apostle, yet at least I am to you; for the seal of mine apostleship are ye in the Lord. 3 My defence to them that examine me is this. 4 Have we no right to eat and to drink? 5 Have we no right to lead about a wife that is a believer, even as the rest of the apostles, and the brethren of the Lord, and Cephas? 6 Or I only and

*Barnabas, have we not a right to forbear working?   7
What soldier ever serveth at his own charges? who planteth
a vineyard, and eateth not the fruit thereof? or who feedeth
a flock, and eateth not of the milk of the flock?   8 Do I
speak these things after the manner of men? or saith not
the law also the same?   9 For it is written in the law of
Moses, Thou shalt not muzzle the ox when he treadeth out
the corn. Is it for the oxen that God careth, 10 or saith
he it assuredly for our sake? Yea, for our sake it was
written: because he that ploweth ought to plow in hope,
and he that thresheth* to thresh in hope of partaking.   11
If we sowed unto you spiritual things, is it a great matter if
we shall reap your carnal things?   12 If others partake of
this right over you, do not we yet more? Nevertheless we
did not use this right; but we bear all things, that we may
cause no hindrance to the gospel of Christ.   13 Know ye
not that they that minister about sacred things eat of the
things of the temple, and they that wait upon the altar have
their portion with the altar?   14 Even so did the Lord ordain that they that proclaim the gospel should live of the
gospel.   15 But I have used none of these things: and I
write not these things that it may be so done in my case;
for it were good for me rather to die, than that any man
should make my glorying void.   16 For if I preach the
gospel, I have nothing to glory of; for necessity is laid upon
me; for woe is unto me, if I preach not the gospel.   17
For if I do this of mine own will, I have a reward: but if
not of mine own will, I have a stewardship intrusted to
me.   18 What then is my reward? That, when I preach
the gospel, I may make the gospel without charge, so as
not to use to the full my right in the gospel.*

In refusing financial support from the church at Corinth,
Paul was not questioning the right of Christian ministers
to receive salaries for the maintenance of themselves and
their families. On the contrary, he established this right,
and states that he renounces it in a particular case only
with a view to the furtherance of his work, or rather, for
fear that otherwise his work might be hampered. He was
concerned lest the Corinthians might accuse him of selfish

motives and thus restrict his influence. His renouncing this right and his refusal to accept such support was for the reason which he explicitly states: "That we may cause no hindrance to the gospel of Christ" (v. 12).

The right to receive or to require support as a minister of the gospel is defended on four or five specific grounds. First of all, Paul is an apostle and as such has a right to all that without question was being granted to his fellow laborers.

His apostleship was attested by the fact that he had seen Jesus. He refers here to no mere spiritual knowledge of Christ, no ecstatic visions experienced by him during the course of his ministry, but to an actual sight of the human and glorified Christ which he had been granted when on his way to Damascus. His apostleship had been sealed by his work at Corinth. If other Christians ever raised the question, surely his readers could not, for he has brought the Corinthian church into being: "The seal of mine apostleship are ye in the Lord."

Therefore, as an apostle, Paul had a right to the support which other apostles were receiving. It was his privilege, if he so desired, to marry and to bring his wife with him on his apostolic journeys, as was the case with the brothers of Jesus and with Peter. Paul and his companion Barnabas would have been justified in refusing to perform manual labor. Support, at least, was due to Paul as an apostle.

In the second place, he defends this right on the ground of the usual customs in human society. The soldier, the vinedresser, the shepherd, all receive wages for their work; why not the Christian minister?

Or, if one objects to these parallels as being merely secular and worldly, does not the sacred law of Moses teach the same? It provides that an ox should not be muzzled when treading out grain. The Lord did not intend by the prohibition to make provision merely for oxen, but to teach men the principle that the laborer should have his reward, that one who plows or threshes should share in what his labor has produced. Therefore, as the apostle had sown spiritual seed in Corinth, it was natural that he should receive material support from the Corinthian church.

Paul still further defends his right on the ground that the church was supporting other Christian teachers. Surely none could have a better claim than he by whom the church had been founded; but while other men burdened the Corinthians, Paul had renounced his claim and had endured hardship and privation so as to give no one an occasion for criticism or complaint, which might have embarrassed his work.

Further still, this right of the ministry to financial aid is established by the fact that Jewish priests were supported by offerings which were brought to the Temple and were allotted portions of the animals sacrificed. Most important of all, Christ perpetuated this law in its application to the Christian ministry and ordained specifically "that they that proclaim the gospel should live of the gospel."

This right so firmly and divinely established, Paul had renounced. He is not now defending it that he may claim it: "I have used none of these things: and I write not these things that it may be so done in my case." Paul would rather die than lose the joy of preaching the gospel without asking any return. The satisfaction of preaching gratuitously was a real reward. It constituted actual wages. For preaching the gospel he could accept no reward, for this was his duty, his obligation, his stewardship. Woe would be upon him if he did not preach the gospel. There was, however, no necessity upon him for preaching without material support; the rewarding satisfaction which he felt in so doing lay in the knowledge that he thereby avoided all possible criticism and hindrance of his work.

Thus Paul illustrates in part the great principle he is proclaiming, namely, that by insistence upon his rights one may possibly endanger his success. Indulgence in a practice which he regards as innocent may destroy a man's influence over others.   Paul is establishing this principle specifically to answer the question addressed to him in reference to the use of meat offered to idols.   A Christian, by such a practice, which is in itself harmless, might possibly lay himself open to criticism; and in determining his course of action he must seriously weigh the possibility of this.

It is the duty of modern Christians scrupulously to apply this principle to present questions of conscience.   A Christian worker needs to consider not only whether his course is theoretically right but whether, in itself innocent, it may be open to such criticism as to jeopardize his work for Christ.   In the previous chapter Paul was insisting that one must refrain from some things which are morally indifferent for the sake of his weaker brother; here he insists that one must at times refrain for the sake of his work.

b. Becoming All Things to All Men   Ch. 9:19-23

19 For though I was free from all men, I brought myself under bondage to all, that I might gain the more.   20 And to the Jews I became as a Jew, that I might gain Jews; to them that are under the law, as under the law, not being myself under the law, that I might gain them that are under the law; 21 to them that are without law, as without law, not being without law to God, but under law to Christ, that I might gain them that are without law.   22 To the weak I became weak, that I might gain the weak: I am become all things to all men, that I may by all means save some. 23 And I do all things for the gospel's sake, that I may be a joint partaker thereof.

For his services as a minister of Christ, Paul had claimed from the Corinthian Christians no material support, no salary, no financial remuneration.   He had done this lest his motives might have been misunderstood and his work impeded.   However, he did have his reward.   It consisted in his sense of independence, in the satisfaction he felt in preaching without remuneration, and in being free from the suspicion of mercenary motives.

However, he was making no selfish use of his liberty. On the contrary, while free from all human control, he was making himself a slave of all men in hope of winning some for Christ. While himself free from narrow scruples, he allowed himself to be restricted and bound by the weakness of others that he might ultimately bring them to the enjoyment of the Christian liberty which he himself so well understood. So far from doing what he had the abstract right to do, he made every necessary concession wherever he saw a possibility of bringing souls to Christ, as he stated: "For though I was free from all men, I brought myself under bondage to all, that I might gain the more."

To the Jews he deported himself as a Jew, keeping their feasts and fasts, observing their customs and vows. To the Gentiles who were without law he adapted himself, not requiring them to adopt Jewish ceremonies, quoting from their literature and even basing an argument upon the inscription on one of their altars.

By way of parenthesis he explains that, in accommodating himself to the Jews, he did not put himself back under Jewish law as being a ground of salvation, but that he observed this law only as a manner of social life, and of national custom, and to avoid giving needless offense to Jews; and among Gentiles, while not requiring of them acceptance of the Jewish ceremonial law, he was never "without law" in relation to God, but was under the law of Christ.

Then further, to those who were weak, overscrupulous, and timid, he "became weak," adapting himself to their scruples and making concessions to their prejudices. In brief, he sums up his conduct by saying, "I am become all things to all men." By this phrase Paul means exactly the opposite of what it means in common speech today. He does not signify any weak compliance with the wrong actions and immoral practices of others. He is not approving the maxim: "When in Rome do as the Romans do." Paul is referring to matters of moral indifference, to weak prejudices, and to foolish scruples. He is answering the question as to the use of meats offered to idols. He knows that there is no reality in idol worship. He believes that the use of such meat is not a question of right or wrong, but he is saying that as a preacher of the gospel it may be wise to refrain from some things, in themselves innocent, so as to avoid offending other persons and thus hampering his Christian work.

He states that it is his principle to adapt himself to the needs and prejudices and weaknesses of all classes of men in order that he may lead some of them to Christ. All that he does is for the sake of the gospel, the full benefits of which he hopes to share.

This principle of the apostle should guide more continually all the followers of Christ, and particularly all who are seeking to lead others to a Christian life. Many innocent practices must be renounced because of the prejudices and opinions of others. Not only must all sinful courses be avoided, but one must consider the possible effect of acts which are morally indifferent. As to questions of conscience, it is necessary to regard this second important principle formulated by Paul: Indulgence may endanger Christian work; therefore be "all things to all men."

c. Striving for the Crown   Ch. 9:24-27

24 Know ye not that they that run in a race run all, but one receiveth the prize? Even so run; that ye may attain. 25 And every man that striveth in the games exerciseth self-control in all things. Now they do it to receive a corruptible crown; but we an incorruptible. 26 I therefore so run, as not uncertainly; so fight I, as not beating the air: 27 but I buffet my body, and bring it into bondage: lest by any means, after that I have preached to others, I myself should be rejected.

Paul was fond of picturing the Christian life under figures drawn from the Greek games. He refers here to these contests, in order to emphasize the need of self-control and self-denial even in matters morally indifferent. In answering the question as to the use of meats offered to idols, Paul has been insisting upon the necessity of refraining from what is in itself innocent in case indulgence may interfere with Christian service. He made it his rule to become "all things to all men," that is, to accommodate himself to the prejudices and scruples of others in order that he might win them for Christ and become partakers with them of the full blessings of the gospel. Here he insists that all who are to share this blessedness must likewise limit their liberties and must practice the same denial which the apostle is imposing upon himself.

His reference is probably to the Isthmian games, named from the isthmus on which Corinth stood. These contests, like the Olympian, Pythian, and Nemean, constituted a great national and religious festival, and every second year drew eager throngs to the city of Corinth. Only freemen could contend in these games, and the contestants must give satisfactory proof that for ten months they had undergone the necessary preliminary training. For thirty days before the contests, all candidates were required to attend exercises at the gymnasium, and only when they had properly fulfilled all such conditions were they allowed to contend in the sight of the assembled throngs. The herald proclaimed the name and the country of each contestant, and also announced the name of the victor, who was crowned with a garland of pine leaves or parsley or ivy. The family of the victor was regarded with honor, and when he returned to his native city a breach was made in the walls to allow him to enter, the purpose of this being to indicate that a town to which such a citizen belonged had no need of walls for its defense. The victorious hero was immortalized in verse; he was assigned a foremost seat when attending all future contests.

In his reference to these games, Paul makes two points of contrast. In the Greek contest, while all the competitors ran in a race, only one could obtain the crown; but in the Christian life the prize was open to all, and all should so run as to win the promised reward.

Second, in the Greek games the reward was a "corruptible crown," a mere withering wreath of olive or of pine, but, as followers of Christ, we are striving for a crown which will never fade, a crown of life, a crown of righteousness, a crown of joy, a crown of glory.

It is in view of such a crown that Paul urges upon every Christian to fulfill the conditions which were imposed upon the contending athletes, and he gives himself as an example of one who is so striving that he may obtain the coveted prize. The conditions are obvious. First of all, there must be strenuous effort. One is not to imagine that the Christian life is one of easy indifference, even in matters where no question of positive right and wrong is involved. One must make a continual effort to so order his conduct that he will not offend those who are weak in the faith, critical, and overscrupulous.

In the second place, one must be definite in his efforts. Paul declared that he was fighting "as not beating the air." As Christians, we must face these questions of conscience definitely and must settle them with the determination and the decision of those who are striving with unswerving aim.

Then, too, one must exercise self-control even in these matters as to which the consciences of Christians may differ. He must even accustom himself to self-sacrifice. The severe training required of the Greek athlete was a picture of the severity with which one must treat not his body, but his bodily appetites, his desires. Paul is speaking here in figurative language. He declares that he beats his body black and blue, that he strikes his body under the eye, that he leads his body about like a beaten boxer. Thus vividly does he paint the necessity of discipline and of subduing and controlling all the appetites which if unsubdued might lead to moral defeat, and make one lose his crown.

Paul states that his own strenuous efforts are being put forth lest, when he has acted as a herald and has summoned others into the arena, he may himself be disqualified as one who has not submitted to the rules of the contest. With a prize so glorious in view, all who have heard the gospel summons should seek with a like earnestness, self-denial, and self-discipline, to run the race, to fight the good fight, that they too may receive the crown which never fades.

3. The Peril of Self-indulgence   Ch. 10:1-13

1 For I would not, brethren, have you ignorant, that our fathers were all under the cloud, and all passed through the sea; 2 and were all baptized unto Moses in the cloud and in the sea; 3 and did all eat the same spiritual food; 4 and did all drink the same spiritual drink: for they drank of a spiritual rock that followed them: and the rock was Christ. 5 Howbeit with most of them God was not well pleased: for they were overthrown in the wilderness. 6 Now these things were our examples, to the intent we should not lust after evil things, as they also lusted. 7 Neither be ye idolaters, as were some of them; as it is written, The people sat down to eat and drink, and rose up to play. 8 Neither let us commit fornication, as some of them committed, and fell in one day three and twenty thousand. 9 Neither let us make trial of the Lord, as some of them made trial, and perished by the serpents. 10 Neither murmur ye, as some of them murmured, and perished by the destroyer. 11 Now these things happened unto them by way of example; and they were written for our admonition, upon whom the ends of the ages are come. 12 Wherefore let him that thinketh he standeth take heed lest he fall. 13 There hath no temptation taken you but such as man can bear: but God is faithful, who will not suffer you to be tempted above that ye are able; but will with the temptation make also the way of escape, that ye may be able to endure it.

Paul has already shown his readers that indulgence in questionable practices may cause others to stumble, and further, that it may hinder Christian work. He now proposes a third principle: Indulgence may imperil one's own soul; therefore "let him that thinketh he standeth take heed lest he fall."

He cites the example of the Children of Israel and shows that in spite of their great privileges and advantages they fell into grievous sin. In view of this fact he warns his readers, and then adds a word of cheer.

In this reference to Jewish history, the apostle declares that his fathers had been "baptized unto Moses in the cloud and in the sea." By following the guidance of that cloud of glory, and by passing through the sea in safety, they had acknowledged Moses as their divinely appointed deliverer, and had pledged themselves to be his followers.

Furthermore, they ate of the manna which was supplied from heaven and drank of the water which once and again came forth from a rock. The rock not only symbolized Christ; Paul identifies it with Christ. All unknown to the Israelites, Christ was with them in the wilderness. He was the divine Agent who ministered to their needs. Therefore, their food and drink were spiritual and sacramental; they were gifts of divine mercy. So the Corinthian Christians in baptism had pledged themselves to be followers of Christ; and in the Supper of the Lord they had been partakers of his grace.

However, in spite of their unique position and mercies the Israelites proved unfaithful; "with most of them God was not well pleased: for they were overthrown in the wilderness." Thereby Paul warns his readers that indulgence in meat which had been offered to idols, while innocent in itself, might become the occasion of severe temptation before which even they might fall.

So for all Christians, indulgence in questionable practices, which in themselves are not wrong, may be the occasion of temptations too subtle to be withstood. Such indulgence may awaken desires and longings which are sinful, and "we should not lust after evil things, as they also lusted."

So, too, indulgence may bring into our lives something which displaces God as the object of our supreme satisfaction and worship: "Neither be ye idolaters, as were some of them."

Then, too, association with them who indulge in these practices may lead us to sins of impurity, or at least to that friendship with the world and to such unfaithfulness to God as were pictured in the Old Testament by fornication.

"Neither let us make trial of the Lord, as some of them made trial, and perished by the serpents." The continual practice of things which are questionable may become the occasion of our presuming too far upon the forbearance of God, of our attempting to see how far we can go without falling, or of testing God, to learn how far he will let us go without punishment or reproof. The murmurings of Israel finally reached the point of actual rebellion and impious defiance. Indulgence in some forms of amusement, not in themselves sinful, and in practices which other persons regard as harmless, may make us discontented with our lives of more rigid morality, until continued dissatisfaction deepens into disloyalty and ends in actual defiance of God.

The whole experience of Israel, Paul continues, is full of instruction for us who live in a different age, in fact, in the closing age of the world. Particularly does it contain a solemn warning against self-confidence and against the foolish supposition that because we have been baptized and have partaken of the Sacrament, we are, therefore, morally secure. "Let him that thinketh he standeth take heed lest he fall."

After this solemn warning, however, the apostle closes the paragraph with a message of encouragement and cheer. Even though Israel did turn from God, even though we are painfully conscious of our weakness, we need not, we will not, fall. Temptations continually assail us, but no fate closes before us the door of retreat. God allows us to be placed in circumstances which are the occasion of these severe temptations, but he always provides for us a way of escape. We should not place ourselves needlessly in positions of peril. We should not choose those practices which are questionable. We should devote ourselves eagerly to the tasks which we know to be ours. We should with all courage and cheerfulness follow those paths which we know to be right. We should live for Christ and seek to walk with him, and then we shall be absolutely secure.

4. PROHIBITION FROM IDOL FEASTS
Ch. 10:14-22

14 Wherefore, my beloved, flee from idolatry. 15 I speak as to wise men; judge ye what I say. 16 The cup of blessing which we bless, is it not a communion of the blood of Christ? The bread which we break, is it not a communion of the body of Christ? 17 seeing that we, who are many, are one bread, one body: for we all partake of the one bread. 18 Behold Israel after the flesh: have not they that eat the sacrifices communion with the altar? 19 What say I then? that a thing sacrificed to idols is anything, or that an idol is anything? 20 But I say, that the things which the Gentiles sacrifice, they sacrifice to demons, and not to God: and I would not that ye should have communion with demons. 21 Ye cannot drink the cup of the Lord, and the cup of demons: ye cannot partake of the table of the Lord, and of the table of demons. 22 Or do `we provoke the Lord to jealousy? are we stronger than he?

To partake of food which had been offered to idols might be innocent. At most it might be regarded as a matter concerning which the consciences of Christians may properly differ; but to eat of such food in an idol temple with idolaters, and as a part of an idol feast, this would be quite a different matter. From actual idolatry, Christians must flee. They should not see how near they can come to idolatry without partaking in it, but how far they can keep from it. At all events, they should not allow themselves to partake of idol feasts. Therefore Paul states his fourth great principle: Indulgence may identify with the world; therefore do not provoke Christ to jealousy.

It is not difficult to apply such a principle to modern problems. Some practices which are merely questionable under certain conditions, under other conditions may be actually wrong. They may in themselves be matters of moral indifference, but when practiced with persons who are godless and in places associated with sin, they may so identify a Christian with the enemies of Christ as to grieve the heart of his loving Lord.

In enforcing his prohibition from idol feasts, Paul argues from the relation which the sacrament establishes between a believer and Christ, and from the moral impossibility of one who is so united with his Lord's being also closely united with the demons which were supposed to be represented by idols and recognized in idol worship.

Partaking of the bread and wine in the Lord's Supper symbolizes the participation of a believer in all the benefits of Christ's atoning work and in the spiritual life which he imparts to all who are united with him by faith. So, too, this joint participation in Christ's work and Christ's life constitutes all believers one; they form one loaf, one body; and of this unity the Sacrament is always a symbol.

Thus, in the case of Jewish sacrifices, the participants share in all that the altar signifies. Now it is true that idol deities are not real, and that idolatry is an illusion. However, behind the idols are the demons they represent, even, to speak figuratively, demons of lust and cruelty and ignorance with which idol worship is identified. Is it conceivable then that one can be identified at the same time with such demons and with Christ? Is it not absolutely necessary to choose either the one or the other? Will not participation in idol worship "provoke the Lord to jealousy"? Are we ready to challenge his anger?   Could we escape the consequences of his displeasure?

The practice of questionable pursuits may become so identified with the spirit of greed and selfishness and godlessness, that to follow it may be to disown our Master and to grieve the heart of the Lord who loves us.

5. THE ESSENTIAL PRINCIPLES
Chs. 10:23 to 11:1

23 All things are lawful; but not all things are expedient. All things are lawful; but not all things edify.   24 Let no man seek his own, but each his neighbor's good.   25 Whatsoever is sold in the shambles, eat, asking no question for conscience' sake;   26 for the earth is the Lord's, and the fulness thereof.   27 If one of them that believe not biddeth you to a feast, and ye are disposed to go; whatsoever is set before you, eat, asking no question for conscience' sake.   28 But if any man say unto you, This hath been offered in sacrifice, eat not, for his sake that showed it, and for conscience' sake: 29 conscience, I say, not thine own, but the other's; for why is my liberty judged by another conscience?   30 If I partake with thankfulness, why am I evil spoken of for that for which I give thanks?   31 Whether therefore ye eat, or drink, or whatsoever ye do, do all to the glory of God.   32 Give no occasion of stumbling, either to Jews, or to Greeks, or to the church of God: 33 even as I also please all men in all things, not seeking mine own profit, but the profit of the many, that they may be saved.   1 Be ye imitators of me, even as I also am of Christ.

Paul concludes and summarizes his long discussion of the use of meat offered to idols by stating the great comprehensive principles which should be applied by Christians to all questions of conscience: Consider what is expedient and edifies, and do all to the glory of God.

He begins by repeating the great principle of Christian

liberty, "All things are lawful." This seems to have been the maxim which had been used in the defense of eating meat offered to idols, and of indulging in other questionable pursuits. In the sixth chapter Paul had insisted that this liberty must be guarded by his readers for their own sake. He now insists that it must also be limited for the sake of others. He returns here to the point from which his discussion began by insisting upon the supremacy of love.

He is saying in effect that a Christian has the abstract right to do whatever is not in itself sinful, but considerations of expediency and of the welfare of others place practical limits upon this liberty. Some things, in themselves allowable, may not be profitable; some things, in themselves innocent, may not tend to the building up of Christian character. One is to consider not only whether a thing is allowable, but whether it is profitable; "it is not enough that a thing be right if it be not fit to be done," and nothing is fit to be done, however innocent in itself, if it is hurtful to another or open to misconstruction. A Christian must not regard his own interest alone but also that of others: "Let no man seek his own, but each his neighbor's good."

This general principle Paul illustrates in connection with the use of sacrificial meat. He advises Christians to purchase food which is offered for sale in the market without raising any questions or indulging in any scruples as to whether it has previously been used in the worship of idols. This is far different from the case of eating meat in an idol temple. What is purchased in the market is purchased not as part of a sacrifice, but as food which God has graciously supplied for the use of man. "The earth is the Lord's, and the fulness thereof," and therefore all food that the earth brings forth or nourishes is the gift of God and is to be gratefully received.

However, in case another person has scruples, the situation is changed. Suppose, for example, that one is invited

to dine at the house of an unbeliever and he desires to go.
He should feel free to do so and to eat what is provided,
without raising any question on grounds of conscience re-
specting what is set before him. However, if someone says
to him, "This is a thing sacrificed in the temple," he should
not eat it, in deference to that person who has informed
him, and for conscience' sake—not for the sake of his own
conscience, but for the sake of his neighbor who would be
misled and injured by his eating.

This course should be followed for two reasons. First
of all, only harm could result from his eating such food
under these circumstances, and so exposing his freedom to
the condemnation of another's conscience. A second reason would be that such an assertion of liberty in the face
of conscientious condemnation would result in positive
harm, for others seeing him ask a blessing over food which
they regarded as sacrificial meat would denounce his act
as one of sacrilege and scandal. Why should one expose
himself to needless abuse? So Paul concludes, "Whether
therefore ye eat, or drink, or whatsoever ye do, do all to
the glory of God." Avoid placing any moral hindrance
in the way of Jews or Greeks or members of the church
of God. "Adopt my principle," he says, "of renouncing
personal advantages and right, and in everything of seeking not my own profit but the profit of the greatest possible
number in order that they may be saved."

This exhortation closes with the verse which has been
printed as though it belonged to the next chapter: "Be ye
imitators of me, even as I also am of Christ."

G. THE VEILING OF WOMEN IN PUBLIC
WORSHIP   Ch. 11:2-16

*2 Now I praise you that ye remember me in all things,
and hold fast the traditions, even as I delivered them to you.
3 But I would have you know, that the head of every man
is Christ; and the head of the woman is the man; and the*

head of Christ is God. 4 Every man praying or prophesy-
ing, having his head covered, dishonoreth his head. 5 But
every woman praying or prophesying with her head un-
veiled dishonoreth her head; for it is one and the same
thing as if she were shaven. 6 For if a woman is not
veiled, let her also be shorn: but if it is a shame to a woman
to be shorn or shaven, let her be veiled. 7 For a man in-
deed ought not to have his head veiled, forasmuch as he
is the image and glory of God; but the woman is the glory
of the man. 8 For the man is not of the woman; but the
woman of the man: 9 for neither was the man created for
the woman; but the woman for the man: 10 for this cause
ought the woman to have a sign of authority on her head,
because of the angels. 11 Nevertheless, neither is the
woman without the man, nor the man without the woman,
in the Lord. 12 For as the woman is of the man, so is the
man also by the woman; but all things are of God. 13
Judge ye in yourselves: is it seemly that a woman pray
unto God unveiled? 14 Doth not even nature itself teach
you, that, if a man have long hair, it is a dishonor to him?
15 But if a woman have long hair, it is a glory to her: for
her hair is given her for a covering. 16 But if any man
seemeth to be contentious, we have no such custom, neither
the churches of God.

It is possible that Paul may someday be discovered as
the great emancipator and protector of woman. Christianity is strikingly contrasted with other world religions in
the position it assigns to woman, and in the assertion of
her dignity and rights; and this is due in large measure
to the influence of Paul, to his teachings as to Christian
liberty and equality, and to his insistence that the distinctions between Jew and Greek, bond and free, male and
female, are done away in Christ, and all are one in spiritual
privilege and opportunity and in their standing before God.

However, such is not the present opinion concerning
Paul. He is pictured as an enemy of women, and by the
leaders of all feminist movements he is regarded with hor-
ror and disgust. The reason for this disfavor is due in

large measure to what he has written earlier in this epistle in reference to marriage and to what he here states as to the subordination of wives to their husbands.

All will agree that most of the instruction which Paul here gives concerns a custom of dress which was merely local and temporary. No one would insist that women today must wear actual veils when attending Christian worship. However, it is the principle on which Paul bases his instructions to which his opponents object, and which to the minds of his friends makes his statement of present importance and of abiding value. The principle is to the effect that the mental and moral and spiritual equality of the sexes is consistent with the dependence of a wife upon her husband and with her loving submission and obedience to him as well.

It was Paul's very teaching of equality which had led to the particular difficulty at Corinth. This teaching had been misinterpreted by certain Christian women to mean that henceforth they were independent of their husbands, and therefore, defying a custom accepted both by Jews and Christians, they threw aside their veils and appeared thus in public assemblies. The veil had been regarded by them as a symbol of dependence and submission. Laying it aside was a declaration that their new status in Christ ended their former relation to their husbands and left them as free and independent in relation to them as though no marriage vows had been taken.

At the present day it is possible that a misinterpretation of the principle of equality is not only occasioning trouble but is a source of real peril. A false insistence upon the independence of women threatens family life and is binding upon women burdens they never should be made to bear.

The matter at Corinth in some regards was not serious. Paul was simply seeking to maintain at public worship an established custom which made a modest distinction between the sexes, and he was insisting upon maintaining this custom chiefly because of the mistaken grounds on which it was being discarded.

He begins his discussion by a conciliatory introduction. He is now turning to quite a distinct series of topics. He had begun his epistle by rebuking the party spirit at Corinth. Then he dealt with three moral issues, and then with two questions of moral indifference, namely, marriage and meats offered to idols. He is now to discuss three questions relating to public worship, namely, the veiling of women, the observance of the Lord's Supper, and the use of spiritual gifts. The treatment of such subjects relating to Christian worship naturally follows the section in which he has been dealing with idol worship and with the use of food which had been offered in idol temples.

As he must administer some rather severe rebukes, he begins by praising his readers for certain favorable reports he has been hearing of them. They have held him in remembrance and have obeyed his teachings. There is, however, one point of propriety as to which he finds it necessary to correct their practice, namely, the failure of women to wear veils, particularly when taking part in the public worship of the church. Insofar as this is done to express independence and insubordination on the part of wives, it is in contradiction to a divinely established order.

The unit of society, according to the apostle, is not the individual but the family, and in the family the husband is the natural head. He is to exercise this headship, however, only in love and with Christian sympathy and devotion. "But I would have you know, that the head of every man is Christ; and the head of the woman is the man; and the head of Christ is God."

Thus in stating the principle of subordination, Paul at once safeguards it from all tyranny and selfishness and cruelty. In the same way that the divine Son is dependent upon the Father and subject to him, so is a husband subordinate to Christ, and so, too, is a wife subordinate to her husband. The principle involves no humiliation, no injustice, no wrong. It recognizes a difference of function and responsibility, but it precludes selfishness, harshness, and unkindness. If the husband remembers his relation to Christ, he will not abuse his relation to the wife he is expected to honor and support and protect and love.

Paul reminds his readers that this principle of subordination is recognized in the common custom of veiling the head. He did not establish this custom, nor did he place upon it this significance. If so understood, it is decorous for a man to worship with uncovered head, and for a woman to be veiled. If she removes her veil with the purpose of showing her rejection of the principle, why go halfway? Why not really uncover her head? Why not cut off her hair and have her head shaved? This would show real independence of her husband, for the former was done by widows, and the latter was customary for women who disregarded the sacredness of marriage.

It should be remembered that Paul is writing of Christians and of married women. The latter is the more evident as he proceeds to illustrate the point in question by referring to the Old Testament story of the creation. Man was created first "in the image of God," and then woman was taken out of man. Man is the crown of God's creation, reflecting his glory; and woman, since she was derived from man, is the glory of man. "Neither was the man created for the woman; but the woman for the man." Reasoning thus, Paul concludes that a woman ought to wear a veil as the sign of man's authority over her, and particularly in public assemblies for worship, for there, according to common belief, angels are looking down and observing the behavior of Christians.

It should be particularly noted, however, that Paul at once insists that the subordination to which he refers is not inconsistent with personal equality, and that the dependence which is real is also mutual, for as woman was created for man, he declares, so man is born of woman, and both alike, in their mutual relations and differing functions, are dependent upon God. Such subordination does not mean inferiority. To each, equal honor belongs.

The principle is finally defended on the ground of instinct and the sense of propriety. A natural sense of what is fitting shows that it is improper for a man to let his hair grow long, whereas a woman's long hair is her glory, and if it should not be taken from her, no more should the veil of which her hair is a natural symbol.

The apostle concludes, however, that if any man is contentious, he does not himself care to argue the principle further. As to the custom of removing the veil, it had not the sanction of the apostles, nor is it the custom in any of the churches.

It is interesting to observe that while the habit of covering the head in public worship is but a trivial custom which obtained in the days of Paul, it is still almost universally observed among Christians. Its real meaning is little understood. Its true significance is almost forgotten. However, the important principle which it once represented is everywhere questioned or rejected in the alleged interests of the rights and liberties of women. It seems to be a tendency of human nature to retain and exalt insignificant forms and petty rules and to disregard or abandon important principles which should abide.

H. THE OBSERVANCE OF THE LORD'S SUPPER   Ch. 11:17-34

17 But in giving you this charge, I praise you not, that ye come together not for the better but for the worse. 18 For first of all, when ye come together in the church, I hear that divisions exist among you; and I partly believe it. 19 For there must be also factions among you, that they that are approved may be made manifest among you. 20 When therefore ye assemble yourselves together, it is not possible to eat the Lord's supper: 21 for in your eating each one taketh before other *his own supper; and one is hungry, and another is drunken. 22 What, have ye not houses to eat and to drink in? or despise ye the church of God, and put them to shame that have not? What shall I say to you? shall I praise you? In this I praise you not. 23 For I received of the Lord that which also I delivered unto you, that the Lord Jesus in the night in which he was betrayed took bread; 24 and when he had given thanks, he brake it, and said, This is my body, which is for you: this do in remembrance of me. 25 In like manner also the cup, after supper, saying, This cup is the new covenant in my blood: this do, as often as ye drink* it, *in remembrance of me. 26 For as often as ye eat this bread, and drink the cup, ye proclaim the Lord's death till he come. 27 Wherefore whosoever shall eat the bread or drink the cup of the Lord in an unworthy manner, shall be guilty of the body and the blood of the Lord. 28 But let a man prove himself, and so let him eat of the bread, and drink of the cup. 29 For he that eateth and drinketh, eateth and drinketh judgment unto himself, if he discern not the body. 30 For this cause many among you are weak and sickly, and not a few sleep. 31 But if we discerned ourselves, we should not be judged. 32 But when we are judged, we are chastened of the Lord, that we may not be condemned with the world. 33 Wherefore, my brethren, when ye come together to eat, wait one for another. 34 If any man is hungry, let him eat at home; that your coming together be not unto judgment. And the rest will I set in order whensoever I come.*

It seems impossible to emphasize too frequently two of the features which characterized Paul's treatment of the questions which had been referred to him by the Corinthian church. The first is his habit of referring all matters, however insignificant and transient, to their underlying and abiding principles. The second is his ability, even in dealing with matters most delicate, distressing, and distasteful, to state some truth in terms of such striking beauty as to make it appear like a precious jewel embedded in a clod of earth.

Thus when Paul turns to rebuke the serious abuses which are attending the observance of the sacrament, he gives the most complete discussion which the Scriptures contain as to the origin and nature and significance of the Supper of our Lord. Furthermore, he records the institution of this Supper in terms of such exquisite beauty that his words are quoted by practically all Christians when they observe this sacred feast.

The abuses which Paul sought to correct were serious in the extreme. They had their occasion in the custom of uniting the sacrament with a "love feast" or common meal of which the Christians usually partook at the beginning of their assemblies. According to the custom, each person brought with him provisions according to his ability. The rich brought much, while the poor brought little or nothing. Thus provision was made for all, and as all partook of this social meal, the supper was in itself sacramental. However, as the meal was begun, or sometimes at its close, the participants observed in simplest manner the memorial Supper which Christ had instituted. The Corinthians, however, because of their spirit of faction, had introduced their divisions even into these sacramental feasts. Instead of sharing their provisions, the rich were guilty of gluttony and drunkenness, while no provision was made for the poor, and they were allowed no part in the feast. Such a desecration of the sacred Supper was a pitiful scandal which Paul found it necessary most seriously to rebuke. His language, however, is restrained. He declares that he believes only in part the distressing reports which have been brought to him. He intimates even that a divine purpose is being served by the divisions which have been manifest, in that those who were loyal to Christ were thus more definitely recognized. Paul reminds his readers, however, that such revelry and excess make it impossible for them to observe what is in reality the Supper of their Lord. He insists that if their real purpose is merely to gratify their appetites, it would be better for them to remain at home. He severely rebukes them for their lack of consideration for the poor, and for their unseemly and disgraceful behavior.

His actual method, however, in correcting this grievous

abuse is that of reminding the Corinthians of the institution of the sacred Supper which they were desecrating (vs. 23-26). He declares that he himself has received from the Lord the sacred tradition as to the origin of the sacrament. This holy Supper had been established on the solemn night in which Christ was betrayed. This very fact emphasized his self-forgetting love for his disciples. Under the very shadow of the cross he had taken bread and wine and had instituted this sacred rite. "When he had given thanks" he broke the bread, stating to his disciples that it was the symbol of his body which was to be broken for them. Likewise he had taken the cup after the supper, declaring that the cup was to symbolize the new covenant which was to be sealed with his own blood, a covenant new in its nature and in its contents, a covenant which was to secure complete forgiveness of sins and an abiding spiritual renewal. They were to observe this sacred ceremony, as often they repeated it, as a memorial of their Lord, and as a token for his suffering and death in their behalf; and they should continue such an observance until he again appeared.

To his impressive account of the origin of the sacrament, Paul adds a solemn warning: "Wherefore whosoever shall eat the bread or drink the cup of the Lord in an unworthy manner, shall be guilty of the body and the blood of the Lord." Paul means that such shameful conduct as he had described was really profaning the sacred feast and ignoring and insulting the body and blood of the Lord which were symbolized by the feast.

Paul is not here warning unworthy persons from attending the sacrament. This might sometimes be needed; but it is a mistake to introduce the thought here, and this mistaken interpretation of the words of the apostle has kept many innocent persons from the table of the Lord, and has caused others needless anxiety and distress. Paul is not discussing the character of the worshipers, but their conduct in worship. As one of the older interpreters properly declared, "The unworthiness of the participant is one thing; the unworthy manner of participation is quite another" (*"alia est indignitas edentis, alia esus"*). Many persons fear that their conscious unworthiness makes them unfit to approach the table of the Lord. All should believe that however great their faults, they are welcome to this table if they come with true repentance and with a desire for new holiness. Paul had no thought of causing distress to tender consciences. He was rebuking the most gross misbehavior; he was insisting that the Lord's table is no place for gluttony and drunkenness.

There is little danger of such offenses today. Yet all may do well to heed the word of the apostle. "Let a man prove himself," let him be certain that he is mindful of the meaning of the feast, let him be sure that he is discerning the deep import of the service, "and so let him eat of the bread, and drink of the cup." It is noticeable that Paul does not correct the grievous abuses at Corinth by abolishing the love feast, or by insisting upon unfermented wine, or by limiting the wine to the clergy, or by making the communion less frequent, but by warning the participants to regard carefully the sacredness and saving significance of the death of Christ.

Paul further declares that the abuses in connection with the observance of the sacrament had been punished by sickness and by death among the members of the church at Corinth. What was the exact nature of this infliction, he does not explain. He does state, however, that it was not merely a divine judgment, but a chastisement designed to lead the Corinthian Christians to repentance and so to ultimate salvation. Those who were to partake of the Supper of the Lord should examine themselves as to their motives and as to their state of heart, and by this self-judgment they would be free from the judgment and chastisement of the Lord which were visited on the irreverent and profane.

Paul concludes his discussion with a practical exhortation. When the Christians met for their common meal they were to "wait one for another." If any man was hungry, he should "eat at home" before coming to the church assembly. They should remember that the sacramental Supper was intended not to satisfy the appetite but to symbolize a spiritual relation to Christ. All who approach the sacred table sincerely sorrowing for sin and earnestly desiring new strength can do so without fear, but with a confidence that the Lord, in whose real presence they can rejoice, is ready to receive, to pardon, and to impart new life and strength.

I. THE USE OF SPIRITUAL GIFTS
Chs. 12 to 14

Most persons will agree that the spiritual gifts of which Paul writes in his epistles were temporary, supernatural endowments granted to the early Christians to assist them in founding the church. Such gifts may no longer exist. However, the principles which Paul sets forth in discussing these gifts apply to those natural and providential talents and abilities which are granted at the present time to equip men for the propagation of the gospel and for the upbuilding and extension of the church.

Paul's mode of discussion was due to the special circumstances at Corinth. These supernatural endowments were being regarded by the Corinthian Christians as ends in themselves. They were being displayed for the pride and gratification of their possessors. The most surprising of these gifts and not the most useful were the most highly prized, and the exercise of these gifts was resulting in envy and vanity and division. To correct these abuses Paul shows in chapter 12 that the purpose of spiritual gifts is the edification of the church; in chapter 13, that the way to exercise spiritual gifts is in love; and, in chapter 14, that the relative value of spiritual gifts is to be tested by their usefulness to the church.

1. THE PURPOSE OF SPIRITUAL GIFTS   Ch. 12

a. The Test of the Spirit   Ch. 12:1-3

1 Now concerning spiritual gifts, *brethren, I would* not *have you ignorant.   2 Ye know that when ye were Gentiles* ye were *led away unto those dumb idols, howsoever ye might be led.   3 Wherefore I make known unto you, that no man speaking in the Spirit of God saith, Jesus is anathema; and no man can say, Jesus is Lord, but in the Holy Spirit.*

The use of spiritual gifts is the third question relating to public worship which is discussed by Paul, and of the three it is the most difficult and important.   The veiling of women and the right observance of the sacrament were matters of decorum and outward conduct; the gifts of the Holy Spirit had to do with the supernatural, mysterious, personal experiences vitally related to the life and growth of the church.   The apostle begins by reminding his readers that before they accepted Christ they were subject to spiritual forces by which they were impelled to the worship of idols.   These idols were dumb images, speechless and helpless, as were the false gods they represented. Christian believers had been led by the Holy Spirit to the worship of the living and true God, who not only could speak and act, but who gave to men by his Spirit mysterious powers of utterance and gracious gifts for the service of his Son.

However, the worshipers of those false gods, in common with Christians and Jews, held the belief that a man might become possessed by a spirit other than his own, and be used as its instrument as it operated through his faculties and controlled his activities.   Corinth was filled with Greek soothsayers and priests who, no less than Christian apostles, claimed divine inspiration and supernatural powers.

In beginning his discourse relative to spiritual gifts, it

was necessary, therefore, that Paul should intimate to his readers how they could distinguish between these manifestations of the Spirit of God and the utterances and extravagances which were allied with pagan practices and beliefs. He states a supreme test, namely, loyalty to Christ. This will characterize every utterance which is prompted by the Spirit of God.

There was a second test, however, upon which he dwelt subsequently. This was the test of sanity. It may be mentioned here, for failure to understand this test was one cause of the troubles in the Corinthian church.

The inspiration of Greek soothsayers and divines expressed itself in a wild frenzy. They gloried in their absolute madness. They uttered their oracles "like the Pythian prophetess with foaming lips and streaming hair." So the Corinthian Christians were inclined to believe that the more one was deprived of reason and self-consciousness, the more truly was he under the power and control of the Spirit of God. It was this mistake which in part had led these Christians to prefer those gifts which were the more startling and to despise those which were the more practical and useful. Paul seems to indicate that the Holy Spirit operates through the illumined mind and quickened vision and active reason of the believer, and that in the case of true inspiration "the spirits of the prophets are subject to the prophets."

Here, however, he dwells upon the first test of the Spirit's operation, namely, absolute loyalty to Christ: "No man speaking in the Spirit of God saith, Jesus is anathema; and no man can say, Jesus is Lord, but in the Holy Spirit."

"Jesus is accursed" and "Jesus is Lord" were the two contending cries of unbelief and of faith, the two infallible signs of a spirit of evil and the Spirit of God. The former cry might have been uttered by some frenzied enemy of the cross who had intruded into the assembly of Christians, but, whatever his wild ecstasy and alleged possession, he could not have been an agent of the Holy Spirit. On the other hand, the humblest Christian, however obscure his station and commonplace his gift, was a veritable instrument of the Spirit of God if he could humbly but sincerely say, "Jesus is my Lord."

Such teaching is of inestimable value today. There are many alleged spiritual experiences and gifts to which there should be applied the test of Christian sanity. Undoubtedly the Holy Spirit does speak to the followers of Christ, and does impart to them gifts for service. To his presence should be ascribed mysterious and frequent impulses, and to his power should be attributed many results in Christian service. However, these supposed gifts and messages of the Spirit should always be tested and vindicated in the court of reason and of common sense. The more truly one is under the power of the Holy Spirit, the more active and alert will be the faculties of the mind and the reason.

Then, too, one's attitude toward Christ must be taken as a test of his spiritual state. No man, however cultured and admired, can be rightfully called spiritual or godly who speaks evil of Jesus Christ.

For this teaching of the apostle it is further evident that the Holy Spirit is an abiding presence with every follower of Christ. Without the power of the Spirit no one can sincerely confess Jesus as Lord. If such confession is made, it is a consoling proof to a believer that the Spirit has imparted a new life and is ready to use him, however few his gifts, to strengthen and aid the church of Christ.

Furthermore, the spirituality of Christian workers is not to be tested by apparent results. Men do differ in their natural gifts. Popularity and praise are sometimes earned by those whose spiritual life is dwarfed and unreal. The true test is devotion to Christ. It is often found in those whose lives are most hidden, whose efforts and struggles are least known, but as they have yielded themselves to the service of their Master, they most truly have been filled with his Spirit.

b. The Diversity of Gifts   Ch. 12:4-11

*4 Now there are diversities of gifts, but the same Spirit.
5 And there are diversities of ministrations, and the same
Lord. 6 And there are diversities of workings, but the
same God, who worketh all things in all. 7 But to each
one is given the manifestation of the Spirit to profit withal.
8 For to one is given through the Spirit the word of wisdom; and to another the word of knowledge, according to
the same Spirit: 9 to another faith, in the same Spirit;
and to another gifts of healings, in the one Spirit; 10 and
to another workings of miracles; and to another prophecy;
and to another discernings of spirits: to another divers
kinds of tongues; and to another the interpretation of
tongues: 11 but all these worketh the one and the same
Spirit, dividing to each one severally even as he will.*

The gifts granted to the Corinthian church were many
and varied, yet they all came from one divine Source and
all were designed for the common good of believers. All,
therefore, were to be regarded as sacred gifts from God,
and all were to be used wisely as intended for the well-
being of men.

In tracing these gifts to their divine Origin, Paul mentions, as one and equal, God the Father, God the Son, and
God the Holy Spirit. With each person in this Trinity he
associates one aspect of the spiritual gifts which had been
granted to the church. As to their quality and source they
are gracious bestowals, talents, abilities. As to their purpose, they are "ministrations" intended for the service and
help and strength of the church. As to their effect, they
are workings or operations or manifestations of divine
power.

These all have a unity in being distributed from the same
source, for the word "diversities" also signifies "distribu-
tions," or, as Paul adds, each is a manifestation of the
Spirit.

The unity exists further in the fact that all serve the one

common purpose of advancing the interests of the church. "But to each one is given the manifestation of the Spirit to profit withal."

As spiritual gifts, therefore, they were designed not for the gratification of the possessor but for the advantage of all believers.

Paul now proceeds to enumerate these gifts. It is not fanciful to suppose that, as some have claimed, they may be divided into three classes: one associated particularly with the intellect, the second with the will, and the third with the feelings or emotions. The word of wisdom and the word of knowledge refer to divinely imparted faculties, first of discovering, and second of making practical application of truth. It is noticed that these gifts are mentioned at the very head of the list as being of most importance. In the estimate of the Corinthians they held the lowest place. These Christians believed that when reason and consciousness were least active, one was most truly under the power of the Spirit. Paul indicates, however, that the highest spiritual gifts were exercised in connection with the exercise of the reason and the intelligence.

Among the gifts which had specially to do with the will, Paul mentions faith as a gift of the Spirit. By this, of course, he does not mean merely "saving faith" in general, for this is not a special gift, but belongs to all Christians. It is the very root of the Christian life and not one of its fruits. Therefore, he refers here to that "assurance in God," to that "heroic daring" which "removes mountains" and is the product of the indwelling and power of the Holy Spirit.

He next mentions gifts of healings, which refer to the miraculous ability to heal different classes of sickness.

He then notes workings of miracles, by which he probably indicates such ability to raise the dead and to expel demons and to inflict punishment upon adversaries as Paul had exhibited in his own career.

By the gift of prophecy and the discerning of spirits,

Paul indicates first of all a miracle in the form of speech, since, as has been well said, "prophecy does not proceed from a resolution or reflection of the prophet's own, but from a power independent of him which masters his mind and makes him speak in order to act on others." However, as there were false prophets as well as true, there was a correlative gift which is defined as "discernings" of spirits. One possessing such a gift was able to determine for the church whether a professed prophet was controlled by an evil spirit or was inspired by God.

The last gifts enumerated by the apostle are the gift of tongues and "the interpretation of tongues." There has been much speculation as to the nature of these gifts. In all probability, the gift of tongues here named was not identical with the manifestation on the Day of Pentecost. It probably did not consist in the ability to speak in known languages, but rather, was "an overpowering influence of profound emotion," which enabled one "to pray, sing, or give thanks in an ecstatic language unintelligible to every one who did not share the same emotion." Thus this gift is peculiarly in the sphere of the feelings and has little effect upon the understanding or will, which at the time seem to be inactive.

Emotions which had been the immediate creation of the Spirit, and had been expressed in such mysterious speech, could be understood only by one whom the Spirit put in communion with the speaker. It would be necessary for one thus gifted to interpret what had been spoken. He must be enabled by the Spirit to explain in distinct words the rapturous expressions of those who possessed the gift of tongues.

It is, therefore, noticeable that Paul places in the very lowest rank the gifts which the Corinthians coveted most. These gifts might be most startling, but they were of far less help in the edification of the church. We are not to regard these gifts as mere varying natural aptitudes but as actual supernatural endowments. They may no longer be granted to Christians, but their counterparts are found in the various and differing talents possessed by the followers of Christ. These too have a common source in the providential dispensation of God and they have a common purpose in ministering to the church. This fact as to their one aim and purpose should remove from their possessors all pride and vanity and should make them realize their great responsibility for seeking the common good and advantage of their fellowmen.

c. The Unity of the Church   Ch. 12:12-31

12 For as the body is one, and hath many members, and all the members of the body, being many, are one body; so also is Christ. 13 For in one Spirit were we all baptized into one body, whether Jews or Greeks, whether bond or free; and were all made to drink of one Spirit. 14 For the body is not one member, but many. 15 If the foot shall say, Because I am not the hand, I am not of the body; it is not therefore not of the body. 16 And if the ear shall say, Because I am not the eye, I am not of the body; it is not therefore not of the body. 17 If the whole body were an eye, where were the hearing? If the whole were hearing, where were the smelling? 18 But now hath God set the members each one of them in the body, even as it pleased him. 19 And if they were all one member, where were the body? 20 But now they are many members, but one body. 21 And the eye cannot say to the hand, I have no need of thee: or again the head to the feet, I have no need of you. 22 Nay, much rather, those members of the body which seem to be more feeble are necessary: 23 and those parts *of the body, which we think to be less honorable, upon these we bestow more abundant honor; and our uncomely* parts *have more abundant comeliness; 24 whereas our comely* parts *have no need: but God tempered the body together, giving more abundant honor to that* part *which lacked; 25 that there should be no schism in the body; but* that *the members should have the same care one for another. 26 And whether one member suffereth, all the members suffer with it; or* one *member is*

*honored, all the members rejoice with it. 27 Now ye are
the body of Christ, and severally members thereof. 28
And God hath set some in the church, first apostles, secondly prophets, thirdly teachers, then miracles, then gifts
of healings, helps, governments, divers kinds of tongues.
29 Are all apostles? are all prophets? are all teachers? are
all workers of miracles? 30 have all gifts of healings? do all
speak with tongues? do all interpret? 31 But desire earnestly the greater gifts. And moreover a most excellent
way show I unto you.*

The wide diversity of gifts granted to its members was
consistent with the unity of the church; in fact it secured
unity; for each gift was designed to contribute something
which was necessary to the common life and growth.

To illustrate this important truth, Paul employs the familiar figure or parable of the human body. It had been
used frequently by Greek writers in reference to the state,
or the "body politic." Paul employs it here with telling
effect.

The church is the spiritual body of Christ. In fact, Paul
even ventures here to identify the church with Christ:
"For as the body is one, and hath many members, and all
the members of the body, being many, are one body; so
also is Christ," (v. 12).

No statement of the unity of the Christian church could
be more clear than this, nor any more startling than that
which follows: "For in one Spirit were we all baptized into
one body, whether Jews or Greeks, whether bond or free;
and were all made to drink of one Spirit" (v. 13). Even
such apparently changeless distinctions as existed in ancient society between Jew and Gentile, and slave and freeman, were done away by the operation of God's Spirit, and
all Christian believers were united in one body by the influence of this Spirit and made to share in one common life.

Many persons today employ the phrase "baptism of the
Spirit" to indicate an experience subsequent to conversion,
or to describe new increments of spiritual power. It is

probably more Scriptural to define such experiences by the phrase, "Filled with the Spirit." There may be many "fillings," but one "baptism." The latter is that initial activity of the Holy Spirit by which the believer is brought into union with the one, indivisible body of Christ, namely, the Christian church to which all believers belong.

Paul proceeds to show that the church is a living organism, as is the human body. There are many members but each one is necessary to the life and well-being of all. The loss of any one member would be a mutilation of the body.

It should be remembered that the apostle is addressing himself to a particular problem. The Corinthian Christians were exaggerating the importance of certain spiritual gifts, particularly that of speaking with tongues. Those who did not possess these more coveted gifts were tempted to be discontented and to deprive the church of the less surprising but no less necessary services which they could render.

On the other hand, those possessing the more brilliant gifts were inclined to assume the more prominent places in the church assemblies and the church service, to the humiliation and exclusion of the less richly gifted.

Both these faults Paul corrects by his use of the parable of the human body. He shows how absurd it would be for one member, a foot or a hand, to refuse to function, and to act as though it did not belong to the body just because it had a different office from some other member, as, for example, an ear or an eye. Just so absurd is it for one member of the church to envy those who possess gifts he lacks, and to refuse to render to the church the service which it is in his power to give.   (Vs. 14-20.)

The second fault is just as foolish. One organ of the body cannot despise the other organs, and declare that it has no need of them; for every organ, however lacking in beauty, is a necessary part of the body, and upon its proper functioning the health of the body depends. So foolish is it for any member of the church to despise any less gifted member and to suppose that his own spiritual life will not suffer if he fails to honor those who appear less brilliant and admirable than himself. (Vs. 21-25.)

These principles are of obvious application to the members of the modern church. They forbid us to envy those who have the gifts we lack, and rebuke us for contempt of those who lack the gifts we have. Such is the message of the apostle as, in the remainder of the chapter, he enumerates the various gifts of the Spirit and enforces these lessons upon his readers.

The list differs somewhat from that already given. (Vs. 8-10.) Here the order is not determined by the essential nature of the gifts as allied to the intellect or will or feelings but by the relative importance of the gifts in the work and edification of the church.

First on the list are the "apostles" with their direct commission from Christ and their supreme task of founding the church; second, "prophets," with their revelations from God, and with their itinerant ministry among churches; third, "teachers," who received the gospel story, explained its content, and applied its truths to practical life. Then there were those who rendered lesser ministries, such as working "miracles," particularly those of bodily healings; those who as "helps" to the poor and the orphans, the sick, and the strangers, brought various kinds of relief; and also "governments," or the proper administration of church affairs. Last of all, and least important of all, came "divers kinds of tongues."

The very order of recounting these gifts may have been a rebuke to the Corinthians for disrespect to the apostle and for their almost childish delight in the spectacular gift of tongues. As these are all declared to be sovereign gifts of God, the real message, however, is this, that no member of the church is unecessary to its life, however small his gift. (Vs. 26-28.)

The complementary truth is enforced as Paul enumerates the gifts again in the form of questions. How did God bestow these gifts? Did he give all to all? By no means, for then each member would have been complete in itself and independent of all others, and the very body would have been destroyed. Thus Paul emphasizes this second truth, that no member of the church is self-sufficient, however great his gifts may be. (Vs. 29-30.)

Such a message emphasizes the mutual dependence sustained by members of the church in view of their diverse gifts and talents, and the duty of each member to exercise faithfully what ever talent he may possess.

In fact Paul closes his discussion with the exhortation to "desire earnestly the greater gifts." If gifts are divine disposals, this exhortation can only mean that by appreciating the gifts granted and by their faithful use, Christians may be prepared for the reception of greater gifts and will be more helpful in the exercise of those they already have. Probably Paul is referring to those "greater gifts" of prophecy and teaching of which he is to write later (ch. 14). He first pauses, however, to speak, in an immortal passage, of the "most excellent way" for the attainment and exercise of all gifts, the way of love (ch. 13).

2. THE WAY OF LOVE   Ch. 13

Paul's matchless message regarding "the way" of exercising spiritual gifts is so superb in its substance, so rhythmic and poetic in its form, that it has become known familiarly as his "Hymn of Love."

Surprise has been expressed that such a hymn should have been penned by this particular apostle. Yet the feeling is due only to a misunderstanding of Paul. He is often pictured merely as a writer of keen intelligence and relentless logic, severe, cold, unfeeling, and austere. In reality he was a man of deep emotions, true sentiment, and devoted friendships, a human being of passion and tenderness and tears. A man void of sympathy and affection never could have won the devotion of multitudes, as did Paul, nor could he have composed the world's greatest lyric of love.

Others have wondered that the words were written by "the apostle of faith," rather than by John, "the apostle of love"; but it should be remembered that these writers were in perfect agreement; each may have laid characteristic stress on one of these graces, yet John declared that "this is the victory that hath overcome the world, even our faith," and Paul made the comprehensive, arresting affirmation that "love therefore is the fulfillment of the law."

Indeed, it is as a grace, and not as a spiritual gift, that Paul is here treating of love. He has been considering "tongues" and "prophecy" and "healings" and other miraculous endowments which were granted to the early church, but here he is showing the way in which these gifts are to be used, and all life is to be lived.

The grace or virtue here considered is not love toward God, which is the highest form of love; not love toward those who give us gratification, which may be merely selfish and sensual emotion; but the attitude of heart and mind toward all mankind which we should cherish and cultivate.

If Paul's beautiful discussion of this virtue is regarded as a hymn, it may be divided into three stanzas which treat of the necessity, the nature, and the permanence of love.

a. Love Indispensable   Ch. 13:1-3

1 If I speak with the tongues of men and of angels, but have not love, I am become sounding brass, or a clanging cymbal. 2 And if I have the gift of prophecy, and know all mysteries and all knowledge; and if I have all faith, so as to remove mountains, but have not love, I am nothing. 3 And if I bestow all my goods to feed the poor, and if I give my body to be burned, but have not love, it profiteth me nothing.

First of all, then, love is absolutely indispensable. Paul shows it to be such in the exercise of spiritual "gifts," and it is such, indeed, in all the activities and relationships of life. The most prized, because the most spectacular, of these gifts to the Corinthian Christians was that of "tongues," or the ability to make ecstatic utterances which were understood only by one who had the corresponding gift of interpretation. Though one should speak with this, the highest form of earthly language, the "tongues" sometimes granted to men, or even with the tongues of angels, the very language of heaven, if the speaker were not animated by love, his utterances would be mere senseless noise, like "sounding brass, or a clanging cymbal."

In the church of Corinth there was much danger of such meaningless utterances because of the prevalent spirit of faction and jealousy and pride. Even in the modern pulpit, preachers and defenders of the faith who possess real eloquence are sometimes so lacking in sympathy and kindness and love that their utterances are harsh, strident, metallic, and thus totally lacking in helpfulness, in persuasiveness and in power.

So, too, although one should "have the gift of prophecy," that special endowment which enabled its possessor to interpret the most profound truths of religion or even to predict future events; and although in order to the exercise of this gift one might understand all "mysteries" of divine revelation and possess all related "knowledge"; although, indeed, one should have the gift of miracle-working "faith" such as our Savior described when he pictured the power to move mountains, nevertheless without love one might be utterly deficient in Christian character.

Today, men may possess knowledge of divine truth and have great ability in the exposition of Scripture, and they may show the most confident faith in God, yet, if they are lacking in love, they are not true exponents of Christian life. They are nothing.

Then again, though one should be so charitable as to

give all his goods "to feed the poor," and though as a
martyr for the truth he should give his "body to be burned,"
unless the real motive which animated him were love, he
would receive no reward. His charity might have its
source in an expectation of recompense or praise, or in a
desire for display and to be seen of men; death at the stake
might be faced in mere fanaticism, in ambition for a reputed sainthood, in stubbornness, or in pride.

A striking emphasis is seen in these successive phrases
which Paul employs to describe the uselessness of prophecy
and faith, of charity and sacrifice of life, unless the one
actuating motive is love. The gift of tongues signifies nothing. The influence of prophecy or faith amounts to nothing. The offering of goods, or even martyrdom, secures
nothing. Love is absolutely necessary if life in any sphere
is to be of value or profit or meaning. Without it no gift
can be exercised properly, no talent can be rightly used.
Without it Christian profession is a pretense, Christian
service is fruitless. Without it all the relations of life are
imperfect, all activities heartless and futile and vain. In
the deepest sense, not to love is not to live.

b. Love Made Manifest   Ch. 13:4-7

> 4 Love suffereth long, and is kind; love envieth not; love
> vaunteth not itself, is not puffed up, 5 doth not behave
> itself unseemly, seeketh not its own, is not provoked, taketh
> not account of evil; 6 rejoiceth not in unrighteousness,
> but rejoiceth with the truth; 7 beareth all things, believeth
> all things, hopeth all things, endureth all things.

Love may be difficult to define; it is not difficult to discern. Paul attempts no definition, analysis, or description;
he pictures love in action. He shows what it does and
feels, and what it refrains from doing. He records the
ways in which it manifests itself. As he does so, he is
noting these manifestations in a restricted sphere, and he
is seeking the solution of a practical problem. He is con-

cerned with the state of the Corinthian church, disturbed and divided as it is by the way in which its spiritual gifts are being exercised and regarded and employed.

Paul has shown that without love spiritual gifts are useless; he now points out how the possessors of such gifts would think and act if they were to be animated by love. He has demonstrated that love is indispensable; he now indicates that love is unmistakable. He has declared love to be necessary; he now reveals its surpassing beauty, and displays its intrinsic excellence and charm.

Not of love in the abstract is the apostle treating, nor is he attempting a complete summary of its qualities or elements; yet what he says constitutes the most perfect panegyric of love ever penned. Although he is seeking only to dispel from the Corinthian church its discords and divisions and strife, he succeeds in revealing as no other writer ever had done or has done what love can do when allowed to rule in any heart or home, in any circle or church, in any community or sphere of the whole wide world.

In fifteen exquisite phrases Paul pictures vividly the operation of a principle which has power to transform all human life.

"Love suffereth long, and is kind." These two comprehensive statements describe the essential operation of love. Love makes one patient in enduring evil, active in conferring good. The evil referred to is such as emanates from provoking and injurious human beings; toward such persons love is magnanimous in the enduring of wrongs. It does not give place to bitterness and wrath; it is long-suffering under injuries. It harbors no resentment. It forgives—not only seven times but seventy times seven.

Love does not return evil for evil. It is kind. It is not merely passive; it is actively engaged in doing good. It does kindnesses. Its kindly spirit is expressed in a certain familiar rule of life:

"I shall pass through this world but once. Any good thing, therefore, that I can do, or any kindness that I can show to any human being, let me do it now. Let me not defer it, or neglect it, for I shall not pass this way again."

"Love envieth not." Itself generous, it does not begrudge others their gifts; and if at any time it is being outstripped by competitors, it harbors no irritation, feels no distress. It recognizes no jealousy when a rival receives the prize and praise.

"Love vaunteth not itself." Humble, not boastful; unostentatious, not anxious to display superior gifts or to attract unmerited admiration—this is love. Love is not arrogant toward inferiors—it is not "puffed up"; love never makes itself ridiculous by immodesty or irreverence or by any air of assumed superiority or sense of personal greatness.

Love "doth not behave itself unseemly"; love is true courtesy. The art of politeness cannot be learned exclusively from books of etiquette; it comes from within; it is inspired by sympathy, and is guided by consideration for the feelings of others. It is commonly a lack of love rather than a lack of knowledge that leads to bad manners, impropriety, and embarrassing rudeness. Indeed, chivalry and courtesy cannot be manufactured by rule; they are the natural emanations of a sympathetic heart. Love cannot wound, love cannot distress, love can give no discomforting embarrassment. Love is adverse to all unseemly contentions; the strifes which were disturbing the church at Corinth were not the fruitage of the courtesy which is love. For courtesy, by its very nature, suggests that it should have its own first expression in the dealings of Christians with those with whom they differ.

Love "seeketh not its own"; it is surpassingly unselfish. It is not the mark of love to be ever insisting upon its rights. Love refrains from demanding precedence, recognition, applause, even the consideration which may rightly be expected. For love is deeper than justice.

Love is good-natured; it "is not provoked." Never is love irritable. That ill temper which has been called "the vice of the virtuous" is often the one serious defect in characters otherwise noble. Sadly marring such nobility, it is indeed a pitiful fault, the cause of unutterable misery and pain. But there is a most excellent way of prevention; the infallible cure of an irritable temper, which reveals a heart dominated by self, is the persevering cultivation of unselfish love.

Love "taketh not account of evil"; it resents not. Storing up the memory of wrongs, of indifference, of contempt, of grievances, of wounds; making a rigorous record of the injuries received from others—this is not the way of the love which is of Christ. Love is able not only to forgive but also completely to forget.

Love creates charity toward all the faults and failures of one's fellowmen. Love "rejoiceth not in unrighteousness," is "never glad when others go wrong," finds no secret satisfaction in discovering the moral weakness or the hidden wickedness of a rival, is not eager to spread an evil report, glories not in the triumph of wrong.

Love "rejoiceth with the truth." When truth prevails, love shares the gladness of its victory. If one considers that the truth here indicated refers to the gospel, he sees that in the progress and vindication of that gospel love finds keen delight. Or if one accepts the more probable meaning and views truth as contrasted with falsehood or righteousness contrasted with iniquity, once again he gazes upon love's triumph. Love rejoices when truth defeats calumny, when suspicions are proved unfounded, when wrong is vanquished and right prevails. "Love is gladdened by goodness."

Love ever is ready to make excuses for others; it throws a kindly mantle over all their faults. Love "beareth all things."

Love "believeth all things" that are good. It cherishes faith even in persons who are under suspicion. Love enables one to bestow an inspiriting trust on his fellowmen and to take them at their highest and their best. And such showing of confidence often has an immediate reward; it discloses, even in the most depraved, unsuspected qualities of goodness and strength.

But what will be the case if dark days come when one is compelled to cease trusting, when what seems the very worst has been at last made plain—what will love do then? Even in such a crisis love does not despair; if no longer it can hope for acquittal, it looks confidently and impellingly for reformation and recovery, ultimate vindication and victory. For love "hopeth all things."

And love "endureth all things," undaunted, undiscouraged, even to the end. Patient even in moments and days and long, long years when hope is deferred, love grows not weary. Under the burden of prolonged delay, it holds fast, hopes on, bravely perseveres, and courageously endures.

These, then, are some of the manifestations of the grace we know as love. It is a grace difficult to imitate, counterfeit, or conceal. More to be desired is it than any gift, however attended that may be by marvel or mystery or miracle. More than the exercise of any gift, its operation would unite and edify the church of Christ. Under its complete control the humblest life becomes a radiant source of strength, of help, of harmony. By its victorious power the enthroned Christ will bring to the waiting world its destined age of glory and of gold.

c. Love Imperishable   Ch. 13:8-13

8 *Love never faileth: but whether* there be *prophecies, they shall be done away; whether* there be *tongues, they shall cease; whether* there be *knowledge, it shall be done away.* 9 *For we know in part, and we prophesy in part;* 10 *but when that which is perfect is come, that which is in part shall be done away.* 11 *When I was a child, I spake as a child, I felt as a child, I thought as a child: now that I am become a man, I have put away childish things.* 12 *For now we see in a mirror, darkly; but then face to face: now I know in part; but then shall I know fully even*

*as also I was fully known.   13 But now abideth faith, hope,
love, these three; and the greatest of these is love.*

Love is immortal. In contrast with gifts and talents
which have their place and purpose in time alone, love is a
grace which through all eternity will continue to manifest
its glorious power. As Paul continues his praise of this
virtue, he now makes definite and contrasting reference to
those gifts of prophecy and tongues and knowledge which
had been granted for the strengthening and guidance of
the Corinthian church.

Love is indispensable in exercising these gifts, the apostle
has shown, and, further, their possession may give fine occasion for the beautiful manifestations of love. Now he
composes a new stanza in his Hymn of Love. He sings
that love is to continue after all these gifts have passed
away. "Love never faileth: but whether there be prophecies, they shall be done away; whether there be tongues,
they shall cease; whether there be knowledge, it shall be
done away."

"They shall be done away." Let it be granted that the
spiritual gifts which had been bestowed on the Corinthian
church were to be confined to the apostolic age. Though
Paul does not here so affirm, this limitation probably was a
fact; it is rather certain that these exact gifts no longer
exist. But the contrast in his Hymn of Love was not between the apostolic age and the present time, but between
the present age as a whole and the future age which is to
be ushered in by the return of Christ. Spiritual gifts were
granted, at best, only for an era which was imperfect and
preparatory, but love, love will continue, love will endure,
love will be indispensable even "when that which is perfect
is come."

In time or in eternity, love will never cease to be. Love
is imperishable. "Whether there be prophecies, they shall
be done away"—not because they are false and untrue, but
because they all have had their perfect fulfillment, and

because in the age to come there will be no occasion, no need for any prophetic gift. But "love never faileth."

"Tongues . . . shall cease," but not love. The purpose of this most coveted gift of tongues was only the producing of a temporary effect and the giving of aid in the founding of the early church. All necessity for its exercise is now gone, and surely in the future state this apparently mysterious form of unintelligible utterance will no longer be desired. But "love never faileth."

"Knowledge . . . shall be done away." How and why, Paul makes brilliantly clear: at the appearing of Christ that which is partial and imperfect will inevitably vanish before that which is perfect and complete. All our knowledge, even such as that granted to the early Christians by special illumination, is fragmentary, temporary, provisional: "Knowledge . . . shall be done away." But "love never faileth."

Into his immortal Hymn of Love the inspired composer introduces just here a double strophe. To make plain his meaning as to the vanishing of temporary gifts, Paul employs two comparisons: a child's knowledge, a mirror's reflection.

A child's knowledge, as every thoughtful adult knows, in due time gives way to the more perfect understanding of mature years: "When I was a child, I spake as a child, I felt as a child, I thought as a child: now that I am become a man, I have put away childish things." Normal human beings grow, progress, develop. Their resulting change in speech and disposition and mode of thought—transformations which the apostle himself experienced as he grew into manhood—forms a vivid picture of the passing away of our present imperfect knowledge, of its merging into mature and complete knowledge, in that glad day when Christ shall be revealed in glory. Then shall our eyes be opened to see the things which are abiding and eternal. Things of time cease to be, but "love never faileth."

Who can fail to catch the significance of the second comparison? The imperfect image reflected in a mirror, how unsatisfactory it is at best, when compared with immediate and perfect vision! "For now we see in a mirror, darkly; but then face to face." While things are as they are, our present apprehension of divine things must be indirect, indistinct. Broken outlines, dim impressions, vague, shadowy, and tantalizing glimpses—how strikingly they contrast with that direct intuition, that instantaneous full knowledge, which we shall enjoy in the future state of glory!

As for mirrors and their faulty reflections, Corinth knew them. The ancient city, indeed, was famed for its mirrors, highly developed instruments made of polished metal. But even their most perfect reflections were dim and clouded when compared with the direct sight of the eye. Our present knowledge of God similarly is dim with baffling mysteries.

We see "darkly" in our present age, as in a riddle, as in an enigma; but then shall we see the Lord immediately, even as now he himself sees us. Never can our knowledge be so complete as is his, indeed, but it will be as direct as his own. In contrast with its present incompleteness, it will be worthy of comparison with God's present perfect knowledge of ourselves: "Now I know in part; but then shall I know fully even as also I was fully known." Present knowledge, which is only in part, shall be done away; but "love never faileth."

Incomplete and partial though our present knowledge be, let us not, however, fall into the fatal error of concluding that it is delusive or vain. What we know now presents great realities as the objects of our faith, and as the ground of our eternal hopes. It does not deceive us. A divine bestowal, it is to be received gratefully, to be developed continually, and to be used wisely. Only by living in its light shall we be prepared for the enlarged conceptions and clearer visions of a celestial day. For our present needs it is sufficient.

Yet so imperfect is our knowledge that it should never become an occasion for vain boasting, for assumed superiority, for pride, or for strife. With all its limitations and imperfections it should not be a ground for envy, pride, division, and debate. Why should one greatly rejoice in the praise of temporary gifts which so soon are to disappear? Rather let us cultivate, let us display, that virtue which will outlive all time, which will make its possessor meet for the highest service of God.

That which is in part shall be done away, but that which is perfect shall ever continue in its triumphant work; "love never faileth."

Rightly called "the greatest thing in the world," love is also the most glorious thing in heaven. That it will outlast the gifts of time, Paul has shown; he now declares that it surpasses the graces which continue through eternity. Not only is it superior to the things that perish, it is supreme among the things that abide. Of the three cardinal Christian graces, love is and ever will be chief. "Now abideth faith, hope, love, these three; and the greatest of these is love." On this confident, exultant note, the apostle brings his exquisite hymn to its climactic close.

"The greatest of these"—in what, then, does this supremacy consist? Not, surely, in any greater permanence possessed by love as compared with faith or hope. By some students of the hymn the word "now" has been taken to imply that at the present time, during the present age, faith, hope, and love are abiding, but that in the age to come faith and hope will cease to exist, and of the three only love will remain. Quite on the contrary, Paul affirms that all are to abide and yet that love ever will be supreme among the three.

Why this preeminence exists Paul does not pause to explain. Earlier in his hymn he has suggested one reason. Faith without love is imperfect; it may be merely the cold assent of the mind, or the inactive submission of the will, and it may lack in warmth of devotion of the heart. Hope without love may be self-centered or impure. But true faith and true hope find their completeness in true and perfect love. Love is their ultimate purpose, their complete fulfillment, their highest aim, their utmost goal. It is the most blessed fruit of faith; it is the greatest good anticipated by hope.

Then, too, in contrast with faith and hope, love has its manward side, as well. Faith may bring one into right relation to God, hope may put one into a right attitude toward the future, but love keeps one in right relation to his fellowmen. Of value in the individual life, it also brings help to others, it strengthens the church, it gives light and gladness to all the earth; love verily is the greatest thing in the world.

But what need to seek other explanations of the supremacy of love? Is not the all-sufficient reason to be found in the one great fact that love is of the very nature of God? Faith and hope and love all are immortal, but love is divine. Faith and hope bring us into right relation to God, but love is of his essential being. God does not believe; God does not hope; he loves. Love is supreme for the one reason that "God is love."

It is in the knowledge of God, and in the recognition of his love, that love for him, and for others alike, has its origin and source and constant support. "We love, because he first loved us." This revealing sentence from The First Epistle of John furnishes us the clue in our continuing quest for love; and to this quest we are divinely called. Paul's matchless hymn was not penned merely to gratify a sense of beauty, to rebuke us for our loveless lives, or to awaken a sentimental regard for a tender passion or a Christian grace; it was written to arouse us to instant and continued action. Inevitably it is followed by the brief, insistent command "Follow after love," press eagerly forward on this supremely excellent way.

Let us renew the quest. No searching, no adventure in all of life, is more noble, more worthy, more rewarding.

For in time or in eternity there will be nothing greater, nothing better, nothing more glorious than love.

3. THE COMPARATIVE VALUES AND PROPER USE OF SPIRITUAL GIFTS   Ch. 14

The gift of tongues is coveted and even claimed by many members of the modern church. Whether this claim is true or false is a question of fact to be established upon evidence. Most persons are convinced that sufficient evidence to support the claim has never been produced. They believe the alleged experience to be a form of hysteria or self-deception or delusion. In any event, it is well to remember that Paul regarded tongues as the least to be desired of all the gifts of the Spirit, and found it necessary to warn the Corinthian Christians against the abuse and improper estimate of this gift.

It would seem that the gift as here described is not identical with that manifested on the Day of Pentecost. The latter gave the power of speaking in foreign languages which were understood by the hearers. The gift with which Paul here deals was manifested in ecstatic utterances unintelligible to either the speaker or the hearers, unless someone was present who had the special gift of interpretation. The speaker addressed God. Overpowered by profound emotion, he would pray or sing or give thanks in forms of speech which he himself did not understand.

Closely allied to this gift was that of prophecy. In both cases the speakers were moved by the Holy Spirit. But the prophet spoke to men. He uttered a revelation. He proclaimed the message which God had spoken to his own soul. The prediction of future events was not essential to his task; it may or may not have been a part of his proclamation; but all that he said was in language which he and his hearers understood. The apostle here shows that the gift of prophecy is far superior to that of tongues, and he gives practical instruction as to the use of both gifts.

This instruction is based upon the contents of the two chapters which precede. The first of these shows that all gifts are designed for the edification of the church, the second that all gifts must be exercised in love. This chapter shows that love for others will influence one to choose in preference to tongues, the more edifying gift of prophecy, and also will determine the proper and decorous use of both gifts.

a. Prophecy Preferable to Tongues   Ch. 14:1-25

1 Follow after love; yet desire earnestly spiritual gifts, *but rather that ye may prophesy. 2 For he that speaketh in a tongue speaketh not unto men, but unto God; for no man understandeth; but in the spirit he speaketh mysteries. 3 But he that prophesieth speaketh unto men edification, and exhortation, and consolation. He that speaketh in a tongue edifieth himself; but he that prophesieth edifieth the church. 5 Now I would have you all speak with tongues, but rather that ye should prophesy: and greater is he that prophesieth than he that speaketh with tongues, except he interpret, that the church may receive edifying. 6 But now, brethren, if I come unto you speaking with tongues, what shall I profit you, unless I speak to you either by way of revelation, or of knowledge, or of prophesying, or of teaching? 7 Even things without life, giving a voice, whether pipe or harp, if they give not a distinction in the sounds, how shall it be known what is piped or harped? 8 For if the trumpet give an uncertain voice, who shall prepare himself for war? 9 So also ye, unless ye utter by the tongue speech easy to be understood, how shall it be known what is spoken? for ye will be speaking into the air. 10 There are, it may be, so many kinds of voices in the world, and no* kind *is without signification. 11 If then I know not the meaning of the voice, I shall be to him that speaketh a barbarian, and he that speaketh will be a barbarian unto me. 12 So also ye, since ye are zealous of spiritual* gifts, *seek that ye may abound unto the edifying of the church. 13 Wherefore let him that speaketh in a tongue pray that he may interpret. 14 For if I pray in a tongue, my spirit prayeth, but my understanding is unfruitful. 15 What is it then? I*

*will pray with the spirit, and I will pray with the under-
standing also: I will sing with the spirit, and I will sing
with the understanding also. 16 Else if thou bless with the
spirit, how shall he that filleth the place of the unlearned
say the Amen at thy giving of thanks, seeing he knoweth
not what thou sayest? 17 For thou verily givest thanks
well, but the other is not edified. 18 I thank God, I speak
with tongues more than you all: 19 howbeit in the church
I had rather speak five words with my understanding, that
I might instruct others also, than ten thousand words in a
tongue.*

*20 Brethren, be not children in mind: yet in malice be
ye babes, but in mind be men. 21 In the law it is written,
By men of strange tongues and by the lips of strangers will
I speak unto this people; and not even thus will they hear
me, saith the Lord. 22 Wherefore tongues are for a sign,
not to them that believe, but to the unbelieving: but prophesying is for a sign, not to the unbelieving, but to them that
believe. 23 If therefore the whole church be assembled
together and all speak with tongues, and there come in men
unlearned or unbelieving, will they not say that ye are mad?
24 But if all prophesy, and there come in one unbelieving
or unlearned, he is reproved by all, he is judged by all;
25 the secrets of his heart are made manifest; and so he will
fall down on his face and worship God, declaring that God
is among you indeed.*

There are two reasons advanced by Paul to show why
love would lead one to choose the gift of prophecy rather
than the gift of tongues. The first is consideration for
fellow Christians (vs. 1-19); the second is the desire for
the conversion of unbelievers (vs. 20-25).

"Be eager in following this Way of Love which I have
been describing," writes Paul. "It will make you not the
less but the more desirous of spiritual gifts and particularly
of the gift of prophecy rather than the gift of tongues; and
this for the reason that prophecy edifies all while the gift
of tongues edifies only the speaker. He who speaks in an
unknown tongue speaks to God and not to men; no one
understands him, although in his spirit he is speaking se-

crets which have been divinely revealed.   But he who prophesies speaks to men words that edify and encourage and comfort.   The one may do good to himself, but he who prophesies edifies the church.   Now I would be glad were you all to speak in tongues, but more pleased were you all to prophesy.   The latter is therefore the preferable gift, unless the speaker can interpret his speaking so that the church can receive a blessing.   What would be the profit of my speaking to you ecstatic utterances unless I accompanied my speech with some clear word of revelation or of additional knowledge or of prophecy or of teaching?"   (Vs. 1-6.)

To illustrate the uselessness of tongues which are not interpreted, Paul draws two analogies, one to musical instruments and the other to human languages: "If flutes and harps, for instance, make no distinction in the notes, how shall the tune that I play be known?   So if a bugle gives no sound that is clearly understood, who will prepare for battle?   So will your spiritual utterances be to no purpose if they are not clear and intelligible.   So it is with language.   Each has a meaning of its own, but if one does not know the language that is being spoken to him, no idea is conveyed.

"Therefore, in your cultivation and appraisal of spiritual gifts, apply to them the tests of utility and helpfulness."   (Vs. 7-12.)

Paul urges everyone who speaks in a tongue to pray for the gift of interpreting it, and he stresses the superiority of worship which is intelligent to that which is merely emotional.   He insists that if he prays in an unknown tongue his understanding is inactive, and he prefers to pray and to praise God with thought rather than with mere emotion. "If prayer is only fervent and excited without being intelligible, how can one who is unable to interpret what is being said make the prayer his own, by saying, 'Amen' to your giving of thanks?   Such worship is sincere, but it is unprofitable to the hearers.   I do not underrate the gift of tongues; I myself possess the gift in the highest degree. Yet, in the Christian assembly I would rather speak five words with my understanding, that I may instruct others also, than ten thousand words in a tongue." (Vs. 13-19.)

There was something childish in the delight which the Corinthians took in the unintelligible rapture of tongues. It was well enough for them to be utter babes in regard to their knowledge and experience of evil, but in their mind, in their power of distinguishing the useful from the useless, they should prove themselves to be men of mature years.

What was there useful in the ecstatic utterance of tongues? It did not edify Christians; and it did not lead to the conversion of unbelievers. This second phase of the inferiority of tongues to prophecy Paul emphasizes by a quotation from the Old Testament. Long ago when the drunken Israelites mocked at the simple message of God through Isaiah, as though it had been fit only for babes, the prophet warned them that the Lord would speak unto them in another fashion. He would give his lesson through the lips of Assyrian invaders and conquerors. Their speech would indicate Judah's doom. God would address them through this strange foreign tongue in retribution, not to arouse the faith of the Israelites, but to confirm and consummate their unbelief.

So the gift of tongues served a like melancholy purpose for those who were rejecting the simple gospel of Christ. It did not bring them to repentance. It rather confirmed them and made them feel justified in their unbelief. It evoked expressions of contempt for the church and its messages. Prophecy, however, tended to awaken and to strengthen faith. (Vs. 20-23.)

To illustrate further this inferiority of the gift of tongues, Paul imagines an occasion on which the whole church assembled and all its members at the same time talked with tongues. Suppose then certain men entered who were to receive their first knowledge of Christianity or who had not accepted its teachings. What would their impres-

sion be? Would they not conclude that they had entered a
meeting of madmen? If the gift of tongues was the greatest gift which any Christian could exercise, as the Corinthians imagined, could its exercise by all Christians be so
disastrous?

On the other hand, suppose that everyone is prophesying, and an unbeliever or an ungifted man comes in. What
is the result? He is convicted by all, he is searched by
all, the hidden secrets of his heart are brought to light, and
as a result he will fall on his face and worship God, proclaiming that "God is among you indeed."

Therefore the gift of prophecy is superior to that of
tongues, not only, as previously shown, because it edifies
the church, and engages the reason instead of merely
arousing emotion, but also, as here illustrated, because it
can safely be exercised by the whole church, and because
it results in the conversion of unbelievers.

In applying these principles to the conditions of the
present day, one would not feel impelled to desire the gift
either of prophecy or of tongues, but to seek a clearer understanding of the relative importance of emotion and reason to Christian life and service.

There may be too much religious fervor and excitement
in some religious gatherings, but surely not in many; and
most churches need to pray earnestly for a new moving
and inspiration of the Holy Spirit in order that the hearts
of the worshipers may know something of the passion, the
joy, the rapture, the exaltation, the triumphant hope, which
was the common experience of the early Christians even
in Corinth.

On the other hand, if men are to be won for Christ, the
appeal must be made not only to the emotions but to the
intellect as well. There should be no longing for unintelligible tongues or for prophetic revelations of truth
not found in Scripture. Yet there should be a yearning for
new visions of Christ and his grace, and earnest prayer
that the Holy Spirit may endow for the gospel ministry

men of apostolic zeal and passion, whose messages may be so simple that the least learned can understand, yet so cogent, so wise, so logical, so intelligent that they make their appeal to the most cultured and the best informed.

b. Rules for the Exercise of Gifts   Ch. 14:26-40

26 What is it then, brethren? When ye come together, each one hath a psalm, hath a teaching, hath a revelation, hath a tongue, hath an interpretation. Let all things be done unto edifying. 27 If any man speaketh in a tongue, let it be by two, or at the most three, and that in turn; and let one interpret: 28 but if there be no interpreter, let him keep silence in the church; and let him speak to himself, and to God. 29 And let the prophets speak by two or three, and let the others discern. 30 But if a revelation be made to another sitting by, let the first keep silence. 31 For ye all can prophesy one by one, that all may learn, and all may be exhorted; 32 and the spirits of the prophets are subject to the prophets; 33 for God is not a God of confusion, but of peace.

As in all the churches of the saints, 34 let the women keep silence in the churches: for it is not permitted unto them to speak; but let them be in subjection, as also saith the law. 35 And if they would learn anything, let them ask their own husbands at home: for it is shameful for a woman to speak in the church. 36 What? was it from you that the word of God went forth? or came it unto you alone?

37 If any man thinketh himself to be a prophet, or spiritual, let him take knowledge of the things which I write unto you, that they are the commandment of the Lord. 38 But if any man is ignorant, let him be ignorant.

39 Wherefore, my brethren, desire earnestly to prophesy, and forbid not to speak with tongues. 40 But let all things be done decently and in order.

The principle which determined the relative value of the gift of prophecy and the gift of tongues, as Paul implies, should be applied to the right estimate of all gifts.   This principle is that of usefulness, of edification. Those gifts should be most highly prized which are most helpful to the church and to one's fellow believers.

It is in accordance with this same principle that Paul now proceeds to give certain practical instructions relative to the use of spiritual gifts in the public services of the church.

He deals more specifically, first, with the use of tongues (vs. 26-28), and second, with the exercise of the gift of prophecy (vs. 29-36), and concludes with a reference to his authority in giving these rules for the exercise of spiritual gifts (vs. 37-40).

Such special instruction was necessary because of the very exuberance and profusion of gifts in the Corinthian church. There was a danger lest the church gatherings should become disorderly and confused. When the Christians assembled everyone was eager to have a part in the service. One would lead in a psalm of praise, one would deliver a sermon, one would attempt to communicate a revelation, one would break out with the ecstatic utterance of a tongue, and one would at the same time interpret. All would try to speak at once, including the women. It was a scene of wild confusion.

The worst disorder was caused by speaking with tongues, when several of these enthusiasts tried to be heard at the same time. Paul, therefore, repeats his fundamental principle for the use of all gifts: "Let all things be done unto edifying"; and as to the use of tongues, he specifies that no more than three speakers at the most shall be heard at any one service of the church, and that these shall speak one at a time. Moreover, whatever is said must be explained to the congregation; and if no interpreter is present, the man with the gift must keep silent in the church, communing with himself and with God.

So, too, even with the superior gift of prophecy, only two or three speakers should be heard at any one service, and if other prophets are present they may prove their inspiration by silently judging whether or not what is said proceeds from the Spirit of God.

If while one is speaking there is something revealed to another who had not been expected to speak, let the first be silent, for by such giving way to one another all can be heard and all the members of the church be benefited.

No one should plead that he is under a divine impulse and cannot refrain from prophesying. This gift is ever under the control of the will. If it is a genuine case of inspiration, it will be exercised discreetly and with brotherly love; for the spirits of the prophets are subject to the prophets.

If a second revelation were a real interruption of a previous revelation, and if the second speaker were truly inspired, then there would have been a confusion due to the divine Spirit, which is inconceivable, for God is not a God of disorder but of peace.

Married women were not to exercise in public this gift of prophecy. Paul had occasion to correct certain disorders of dress; he now refers to certain improprieties of speech which had appeared in the church. He here argues from the same ground, namely, the headship of the husband, and the dependence of the wife. The authoritative teaching in the church and the public exercise of the gift of prophecy were for husbands and not for wives. The latter should not even interrupt the service by speaking, under the pretense of asking questions. These questions should be asked of their husbands at home. It would be improper for married women to take the place of their husbands in the prophetic office of the church.

Paul concludes by a rather severe insistence upon the authority of his instructions. If the Corinthians were not willing to submit to them, was it due to the fact, he asks, that they felt themselves to be the originators and the sole possessors of Christianity, who alone had a right to determine its rightful demands? Furthermore, he adds, the best proof that a man is a prophet or possessed of spiritual gifts will be found in the fact that he recognizes as the commands of Christ all that Paul is writing. If, however, from ignorant vanity and rivalry anyone willfully rejects Paul's instructions, the apostle refuses to argue with him; let him bear the responsibility and consequences of his ignorance.

As to the whole matter of the relative importance of tongues and prophecy, the former gift is not to be disused or despised, although the latter is more earnestly to be desired; but in any case, the great rule for the church services is to be this: Let all things be done in a becoming and an orderly manner.

The gift of tongues may have ceased, the gift of prophecy may have been done away; yet the injunctions of the apostle contain implications of abiding value. On the one hand, there is a danger that one man in the discharge of his pastoral office may fail to develop the gifts of other persons who might be of real help in the public service of the church. On the other hand, while the public worship of the church should have more of passion and emotion, it must always be governed by reason, and characterized by seemliness, by dignity, and by order.

J. THE RESURRECTION OF THE DEAD
Ch. 15

To the mind of the Greek philosopher the very idea of a bodily resurrection was grotesque and absurd. When proclaimed by Paul at Athens it had been received with ridicule, and at Corinth it seems to have been regarded with similar contempt. At least there were those among the members of the church who denied the doctrine of the resurrection of the dead. One can almost be grateful for this expression of unbelief, for it became the occasion of a discourse which is one of Paul's noblest achievements, one of the supreme masterpieces of literature.

In reading this chapter, two or three facts should be

borne in mind. First, it should be noted that Paul is discussing the resurrection of the body and not the immortality of the soul. The latter fact is always assumed in Scripture, as it is here in Paul's argument. The two facts are closely related. If the first is true, the second needs no proof, and in Paul's discussion it is taken for granted that the resurrection of the body implies conscious and ever-blessed immortality for the soul. However, the two ideas are distinct. The Greeks shared the belief of all races that the soul survives death, but they could not conceive of resurrection. That the soul, which at death is separated from the body, is again to be clothed and is to inhabit an immortal body, is a unique doctrine, peculiar to Christianity and quite distinct from the belief in the transmigration of souls taught in other faiths, or from the dim and ghostly vision of the "after life" held by the Greeks. In this chapter Paul is not discussing whether or not the soul persists after death, but whether it is to be reembodied.

In the second place, it must be remembered that Paul is here dealing with the resurrection of Christians and not of unbelievers. As our Savior distinctly taught, all the dead are to "come forth; they that have done good, unto the resurrection of life; and they that have done evil, unto the resurrection of judgment"; or, as Paul declares, "There shall be a resurrection both of the just and unjust." Whether these two resurrections will be at the same time has been questioned; but Paul is here concerned only with the resurrection of those who are Christ's, "at his coming."

This then is the third important fact to consider as the chapter is read: the apostle is describing an event which will take place at the Second Advent, at the personal reappearing of Christ. As to the experience of believers between death and resurrection, the Scriptures are peculiarly silent. It is difficult if not impossible to conceive of a disembodied spirit. However, we are told that to be "absent from the body" is to be "at home with the Lord." We are further assured that "to depart" is to "be with Christ" which is "far better." Yet this disembodied state is not the final or perfect state. At the return of Christ the soul of the Christian is to be clothed with an immortal body like the glorious body of the risen and ascended Christ. This teaching, therefore, differs from the belief that the soul sleeps from the time of death until the day of resurrection. It also corrects the conception that at death the soul exchanges a mortal for an immortal body. At death the believer does enter a state of blessedness in conscious fellowship with Christ, but the consummation of glory begins at the return of Christ, and with the resurrection of the body.

In his treatment of this doctrine, Paul deals first with the fact or reality of resurrection (vs. 1-34), and, secondly, with its mode or nature (vs. 35-58).

In establishing the fact, he affirms the resurrection of Christ (vs. 1-11), and shows that this makes the denial of resurrection impossible (vs. 12-19), and assures the resurrection of believers (vs. 20-28), and also has practical bearings upon their present lives (vs. 29-34).

In dealing with the mode of resurrection, he discussses first the nature of the resurrection (vs. 35-49), and then the change to be experienced by living and dead at the return of Christ (vs. 50-58).

1. THE FACT OF RESURRECTION   Ch. 15:1-34

a. *The Resurrection of Christ   Ch. 15:1-11*

1 Now I make known unto you, brethren, the gospel which I preached unto you, which also ye received, wherein also ye stand, 2 by which also ye are saved, if ye hold fast the word which I preached unto you, except ye believed in vain. 3 For I delivered unto you first of all that which also I received: that Christ died for our sins according to the scriptures; 4 and that he was buried; and that he hath been raised on the third day according to the scriptures; 5 and that he appeared to Cephas; then to the twelve; 6 then he appeared to above five hundred brethren at once, of whom the greater part remain until now, but some are fallen asleep; 7 then he appeared to James; then to all the apostles; 8 and last of all, as to the child untimely born, he appeared to me also. 9 For I am the least of the apostles, that am not meet to be called an apostle, because I persecuted the church of God. 10 But by the grace of God I am what I am: and his grace which was bestowed upon me was not found vain; but I labored more abundantly than they all: yet not I, but the grace of God which was with me. 11 Whether then it be I or they, so we preach, and so ye believed.

In establishing the doctrine of the resurrection of the body, Paul rests his whole argument upon the undisputed fact of the resurrection of Christ. He tells the Corinthian Christians that he is to remind them of this fact and also is to intimate its relation to other great truths of the Christian faith and specifically to that of the resurrection of the body. These truths he declares to be essential elements of the gospel he had preached, which they had received, which they still hold, and upon which, if it is a valid gospel, their salvation depends.

Chief among these facts which he had received, either by tradition or revelation, were these: the death of Christ for our sins, as the Scriptures had predicted; his burial; his resurrection on the third day as predicted; and his visible appearances to his chosen witnesses.

Here Paul specifies that this death of Christ was "for our sins," that is, in behalf of our sins, to expiate them, that we might be forgiven for them and delivered from them. This the sacred Scriptures had foretold by typical sacrifices and institutions, by psalm and prophecy.

The fact that "he was buried" is here specified to indicate not only the reality of his death but also the reality of his resurrection. The readers are reminded of the empty tomb. Only resurrection can account for that. Christ had not merely swooned; "Christ died." If he was not again alive, if his resurrection was a falsehood or a delusion, why not find his body in the grave, where he was buried?

He was "raised on the third day," as the Scriptures had foretold and as competent and sufficient witnesses attested. Of the appearances of the risen Christ to these witnesses Paul mentions six.

He omits the name of Mary of Magdala and first mentions Peter as being more widely known, especially at Corinth. To Peter who had denied him, to Peter first of all, to Peter all alone, the risen Christ appeared. A sacred silence conceals the time and place and the words which were spoken. They must have been words of pardon; and this experience must have done more to transform Simon into Peter, the man of "rock," than all the previous years of fellowship with Christ; at least he is here called "Cephas," the prophetic name given by Christ.

Paul next mentions the appearance to "the twelve" in the upper room, when Thomas was absent, and when Jesus ate with the disciples and assured them that they were looking upon no disembodied spirit but upon a body which actually had been raised from the dead.

"Then he appeared to above five hundred brethren at once," on the mountain in Galilee where before his death he had promised to meet his disciples, and where he gave them a great commission to make disciples of all nations.

One man, like Peter, might have been the victim of a dream or a delusion, when he thought he saw the risen Christ. It is much less possible that the Twelve could all have been deceived; and when "above five hundred" men all agree in their testimony, the fact to which they witness is not open to reasonable doubt.

"Then he appeared to James," his own brother, who had not believed in him, whose testimony is for this reason the more valuable, whose future leadership in the church at Jerusalem shows the transforming power of trust in a risen Christ.

"Then to all the apostles" he appeared, when Thomas was present, patron saint of all those skeptics whose stubborn doubts have been removed by the vision of a risen

Christ, in whose presence they have reechoed the words of the apostle: "My Lord and my God."

"Last of all," writes Paul, "he appeared to me also." It was when he was on his way to Damascus, and that appearance, which, like all the others, was a visible appearance, so suddenly transformed Saul the persecutor into Paul the apostle that he here compares himself to a "child untimely born." He thus contrasts himself with the other apostles who more gradually and naturally matured from disciples, by years of nurture, into fully developed messengers of Christ.

As he recalls his deeds as a persecutor, Paul declares himself "the least of the apostles" and "not meet to be called an apostle." However, he is not unmindful of the fact that by the grace of God his labors have surpassed those of all the others. Nor does his witness to the resurrection here form an anticlimax. It is the most telling of all the testimonies; and for the very two facts he is mentioning. First, he was a persecutor of the church; how then can one account reasonably for the startling fact that so suddenly he began to preach the gospel and to support and extend the church? Secondly, how explain the fact that the peresecutor came to surpass all others in apostolic fervor and success? There is only one explanation: his vision of the risen Lord.

As to the great fact of the resurrection of Christ the testimony is absolutely united. "Whether then it be I or they, so we preach, and so ye believed." No fact could be better attested, none more reasonably believed. And this fact is fundamental in the gospel which the apostles preached and which the Christian church has ever believed.

b. A Refutation of the Denial of Resurrection
Ch. 15:12-19

12 Now if Christ is preached that he hath been raised from the dead, how say some among you that there is no

resurrection of the dead?   13 But if there is no resurrection
of the dead, neither hath Christ been raised: 14 and if
Christ hath not been raised, then is our preaching vain,
your faith also is vain.   15 Yea, and we are found false
witnesses of God; because we witnessed of God that he
raised up Christ: whom he raised not up, if so be that the
dead are not raised.   16 For if the dead are not raised,
neither hath Christ been raised: 17 and if Christ hath not
been raised, your faith is vain; ye are yet in your sins.   18
Then they also that are fallen asleep in Christ have per-
ished.   19 If we have only hoped in Christ in this life, we
are of all men most pitiable.

It is not certain that any Corinthian Christians denied
the resurrection of Christ; but Paul's massing of proofs
for this doctrine intimates that it needed some reinforce-
ment.   However, there were those who denied the resurrection of believers, who, in fact, denied that there was any
such thing as resurrection.

Therefore, when the apostle has established the fact of
Christ's resurrection, he points out the impossibility of
believing this fact while at the same time asserting that
there is no resurrection, for "if the dead are not raised,
neither hath Christ been raised."   He then shows that the
denial of Christ's resurrection would give the lie to the
whole apostolic testimony, indeed to the whole system of
Christian faith.

In detailing the consequences of such a denial, he mentions (1) that it would make the gospel message, "our
preaching," vain.   This would be emptied of its content,
for the resurrection of Christ was the very substance of the
good news.   The message would be void, hollow, and
therefore "false."

Furthermore, (2) the Christian faith would likewise be
a delusion, "vain," without substance; or, as built upon
the alleged fact of the resurrection of Christ, it would be
undermined.

Accordingly (3) the apostles would be proved to be

"false witnesses," and this, too, of a very serious character, for they would be found to have been giving lying testimony about God, the worst kind of imposture, for Paul had ascribed to God the resurrection of Christ.

Then again (4) the faith of believers would be "vain," not merely in the former sense of being emptied of its content, but in the sense of its being futile, ineffectual. If Christ's resurrection is unreal, then the effects ascribed to it are unreal. Christians are not saved. More specifically, (5) they are yet in their sins. For, if Christ did not rise, then he is a condemned, not a justified Christ, and surely he could not secure the justification of believers. It would follow, therefore, (6) that dead saints "have perished." They fell asleep trusting in Christ and confident of a blessed immortality, but they have awakened to find that they are in perdition, under the condemnation of God.

Then (7) as to living Christians, if with all their sacrifices and privations, they have in this life only a hope resting on Christ, only a hope and nothing more, only a hope which is never to be fulfilled, a false hope of present salvation and of future glory, then they are of all men most to be pitied.

It thus appears that the resurrection of the dead is no mere dream, nor a doctrine to be lightly rejected. If it falls, the whole system of Christian faith falls with it, the resurrection of Christ and the salvation he has secured. However, replacing the foundation, which for the moment Paul had in imagination removed, he builds again upon it the majestic structure of Christian belief as it rises into the mists of infinite and eternal blessedness for believers and for the whole universe of God.

c. An Assurance of the Resurrection of Believers
Ch. 15:20-28

20 But now hath Christ been raised from the dead, the firstfruits of them that are asleep. 21 For since by man

came death, by man came *also the resurrection of the dead.
22 For as in Adam all die, so also in Christ shall all be
made alive. 23 But each in his own order: Christ the firstfruits; then they that are Christ's, at his coming. 24 Then*
cometh *the end, when he shall deliver up the kingdom to
God, even the Father; when he shall have abolished all
rule and all authority and power. 25 For he must reign,
till he hath put all his enemies under his feet. 26 The last
enemy that shall be abolished is death. 27 For, He put all
things in subjection under his feet. But when he saith, All
things are put in subjection, it is evident that he is excepted
who did subject all things unto him. 28 And when all
things have been subjected unto him, then shall the Son
also himself be subjected to him that did subject all things
unto him, that God may be all in all.*

With a note of triumph Paul turns to the positive phase
of his argument. In contrast with the dire and dreadful
supposition of what would be true if there were no such
thing as resurrection, he states the blessed consequences
of Christ's resurrection. It assures the resurrection of believers and the fulfillment of the whole redemptive purpose
of God.

Christ is declared to be "the firstfruits of them that are
asleep." The first ripened grain, or the first sheaf presented to God at the Passover, was a pledge and a sample
of the coming harvest. So the risen Christ is but the first
of the great multitude who are to rise from the dead. His
resurrection is a divine promise and example of theirs.
They are described as those "that are asleep," the reference being to the sleep of the body in death. The soul does
not sleep, but is in conscious fellowship with Christ. It is
with the resurrection of the body that Paul is here concerned.

He declares this resurrection will be due to the power of
Christ and in virtue of the relation of believers to him.
Just as all who by nature are related to Adam are subject
to death, so all who by faith are united with Christ are

certain to be delivered from its power. Death is here described not as a necessity of finite being, but as a calamity which man has brought upon himself, from which he is to be delivered by virtue of the resurrection victory of Christ.

"There is a divinely arranged order: First, the resurrection of Christ, the type and pledge of resurrection; then the resurrection of his followers at his advent; then the end when he will present his perfected Kingdom to his Father."

When Paul says, "Each in his own order," he employs a striking military term. Each comes in his own division, as though the great Captain came first, then the glorious company of his followers, and then the rest of the dead.

"Then cometh the end," not at the same time as the advent, but next in order. "Later on, comes the end." This epoch is described as the time "when he shall deliver up the kingdom to God, even the Father; when he shall have abolished all rule and all authority and power." "The interval between the advent and the end" will be used to bring to its perfection the Kingdom of Christ; "we must, therefore, regard the reign of Christ as the whole state of things which follows the advent and which will last till the epoch called the end." Also "there is to be a sequence in the resurrection of the dead. . . . (1) Christ himself, the firstfruits; (2) the faithful in Christ at his coming; (3) all the rest of mankind at the end, when the final judgment takes place."

The reign of Christ is consummated in the resurrection of the dead. "The last enemy that shall be abolished is death." Before, death was described as a servant of the believer (ch. 3:22). Both are true. Death does draw aside the curtain and usher the redeemed soul into the presence of the Lord. However, death is the enemy whose victory over the body is the occasion of anguish, of separation, and of tears; but at the resurrection "when this corruptible shall have put on incorruption," then will it be true that "death is swallowed up in victory." Resurrection will abolish death.

The deliverance of the Kingdom unto God, and the subjection of the Son to the Father, do not mean that Christ is to cease to reign, or that he is not divine. "It affirms no other subjection of the Son than is involved in Sonship. This implies no inferiority of nature, no extrusion from power, but the free submission of love which is the essence of the filial spirit."

The death of Christ, the resurrection of Christ, the reign of Christ, are all designed to bring to its consummation the redeeming purpose of the Father, and to lead men into fellowship with him who is everywhere present, whose will is ever supreme, the God who is "all in all."

d. The Practical Applications   Ch. 15:29-34

29 Else what shall they do that are baptized for the dead? If the dead are not raised at all, why then are they baptized for them? 30 why do we also stand in jeopardy every hour? 31 I protest by that glorying in you, brethren, which I have in Christ Jesus our Lord, I die daily. 32 If after the manner of men I fought with beasts at Ephesus, what doth it profit me? If the dead are not raised, let us eat and drink, for to-morrow we die. 33 Be not deceived: Evil companionships corrupt good morals. 34 Awake to soberness righteously, and sin not; for some have no knowledge of God: I speak this *to move you to shame.*

Having established the doctrine of the resurrection, Paul pauses to apply the doctrine to his readers and to remind them that it is associated with their most sacred hopes. Here again he adopts the method of indicating what would be lost by the denial of the doctrine; and his practical applications of the truth may be stated as follows: (1) Baptism for the dead is not unreasonable; (2) sacrifice in Christian service is not madness; (3) sensualism is folly; (4) association with doubters is perilous.

As to what is indicated by baptism for the dead there is a wide diversity of opinion. It can hardly mean a vicarious baptism, where one confessed the name of Christ with the view of saving a friend who had died in unbelief. Nor can it refer to accepting baptism for a believer who had died without receiving baptism. There is no proof that such practices obtained in the days of the apostle.

The most probable interpretation is that when unbelievers, bereaved of loved ones, turned to Christ in their loneliness, moved by the hope of a blessed reunion, their expectation would not prove to have been a fond delusion. Their baptism, due first of all to strong human affection, was a touching evidence of their faith in the future life which was inseparable from the resurrection.

In view of such blessed certainty, it was not madness for Christian workers continually to expose themselves to danger and to death. Such was Paul's course of life. Every day he was at the point of death from peril and hardship. If there were no future rewards, no blessed immortality, why, humanly speaking, had he "fought with beasts at Ephesus"? It is quite improbable that he had been placed in the arena; but he had been compelled to contend with fierce and bloodthirsty men. How then would he be recompensed if the resurrection is a delusion and a dream?

On this latter supposition, one might be justified in adopting the foolish philosophy of sensualism: "Let us eat and drink, for to-morrow we die." That was what men were commonly saying in Corinth. It is a commonplace maxim today: "A short life and a merry one." In the light of immortality and future glory, its folly is apparent.

However, many of the Corinthians seem to have been influenced by this Epicurean view. It was due to their intimacies with pagan associates. Paul, therefore, warns his readers against the perils of fellowship with those who doubt the essential truths of Christianity such as the resurrection. "Evil companionships corrupt good morals," writes the apostle, in language which seems to have been proverbial. Then he adds: "Arouse yourselves from the stupor which this denial has produced. Do not yield to the evil influences of those by whom the denial is being made. Their boasted knowledge is really ignorance of God." Thus Paul would put to shame his doubting readers. Thus again he emphasizes the essential importance of the belief in the resurrection. Thus he warns all the followers of Christ that faith determines conduct, and that those who would keep clear their consciousness of God must hold fast to the truths which God has revealed.

2. THE NATURE OF THE RESURRECTION
Ch. 15:35-58

a. The Resurrection Body   Ch. 15:35-49

35 But some one will say, How are the dead raised? and with what manner of body do they come? 36 Thou foolish one, that which thou thyself sowest is not quickened except it die: 37 and that which thou sowest, thou sowest not the body that shall be, but a bare grain, it may chance of wheat, or of some other kind; 38 but God giveth it a body even as it pleased him, and to each seed a body of its own. 39 All flesh is not the same flesh: but there is one flesh *of men, and another flesh of beasts, and another flesh of birds, and another of fishes. 40 There are also celestial bodies, and bodies terrestrial: but the glory of the celestial is one, and the* glory *of the terrestrial is another. 41 There is one glory of the sun, and another glory of the moon, and another glory of the stars; for one star differeth from another star in glory. 42 So also is the resurrection of the dead. It is sown in corruption; it is raised in incorruption: 43 it is sown in dishonor; it is raised in glory: it is sown in weakness; it is raised in power: 44 it is sown a natural body; it is raised a spiritual body. If there is a natural body, there is also a spiritual* body. *45 So also it is written, The first man Adam became a living soul. The last Adam be-*came *a life-giving spirit. 46 Howbeit that is not first which*

*is spiritual, but that which is natural; then that which is
spiritual. 47 The first man is of the earth, earthy: the second man is of heaven. 48 As is the earthy, such are they
also that are earthy: and as is the heavenly, such are they
also that are heavenly. 49 And as we have borne the image of the earthy, we shall also bear the image of the
heavenly.*

Paul has established the certainty of resurrection. He
now turns to consider its nature or manner. First he deals
with the character of the resurrection body; and then with
the change to be produced in the bodies of living and dead
at the coming of Christ.

He opens his discussion with two questions, which some
opponent of the doctrine, or some sincere inquirer, is supposed to ask: "How are the dead raised? and with what
manner of body do they come?" The first question implies that resurrection is impossible; the second, that it is
inconceivable. He replies to the questioner by calling him
foolish, or thoughtless. If he would only use his reason,
he would find an answer as he looked out upon the fields
of growing grain. Each seed passed through death and
decay to a higher life in the form of a plant. True, the
seed does not so literally die as does the body, but it ceases
to exist in the form of a seed to appear in the higher form
of the fruitful stalk.

Such an analogy does not prove the resurrection. It
does answer the difficulty proposed by showing a process
by which God does accomplish what appears impossible,
and, according to his established law, makes the same life
appear in a more glorious form.

Paul further shows the wide variety of forms in which
animal life exists; and declares that there is likewise a
great difference between the bodies of the inhabitants of
heaven and earth, just as there are varying degrees of
splendor in sun and moon and stars. God therefore is
able to provide that form of body which will be adapted
to the needs of an immortal soul.

The apostle does not attempt to describe the resurrection body but from what he here says and from what follows it is evident (1) that this is a different body from the body which dies and is buried. There is no intimation that it will be composed of the same material particles. In fact, quite the reverse is taught. It is to be far more glorious. The natural body is subject to decay, to dishonor, to weakness; the resurrection body will be free from all these limitations and imperfections, a glorious body, perfectly adapted to the needs of the glorified spirit, just as the mortal body is designed to meet the needs of this present human life.

The sowing in "corruption, . . . dishonor, . . . weakness," does not refer to burial. The present life is the seedtime, and the mortal body, out of which, after death, a different body will spring, is in its germinal state.

(2) The resurrection body, therefore, while different from the mortal body will be identical with it. How this identity is preserved the apostle does not state. The identity of the body of a boy with his body when he has become a man is a possible analogy. Every material particle has been displaced, yet the body is the same body. So it is with the resurrection body: "different yet the same is one of the paradoxes of the Christian faith." The body of glory can be traced back to the body of the grave as its conditioning clue. Deathless, perfect, immortal, its nature will be determined in some way by the body of corruption, dishonor, and weakness. Paul is not writing of a new creation, but of a resurrection, a rebirth, and a reappearance.

(3) The resurrection body is to be produced by the power of Christ, and it is to bear his image. It is not the reconstruction of the body of the grave; nor is it the development of an indestructible germ which is in the "natural body"; nor is it the product of a natural force now residing within the human body; nor is it an ethereal "astral body" by which the natural body is at present in-

dwelt. The resurrection body is the product of divine power. It is a glorious repetition of the body of the grave, yet its pattern and form are found in the body of the risen and glorified Christ.

The first man, Adam, became by a divine creative act, "a living soul"; the last Adam, Jesus Christ, in virtue of his own resurrection, has become "a life-giving spirit."

This, too, is the inevitable order. First, as the descendants of Adam we are made like him, living souls inhabiting mortal bodies, and bearing the image of an earthly parent; but as the followers of Christ we are yet to be clothed with immortal bodies and to bear the image of our heavenly Lord.

b. The Change of Dead and Living   Ch. 15:50-58

50 Now this I say, brethren, that flesh and blood cannot inherit the kingdom of God; neither doth corruption inherit incorruption. 51 Behold, I tell you a mystery: We all shall not sleep, but we shall all be changed, 52 in a moment, in the twinkling of an eye, at the last trump: for the trumpet shall sound, and the dead shall be raised incorruptible, and we shall be changed. 53 For this corruptible must put on incorruption, and this mortal must put on immortality. 54 But when this corruptible shall have put on incorruption, and this mortal shall have put on immortality, then shall come to pass the saying that is written, Death is swallowed up in victory. 55 O death, where is thy victory? O death, where is thy sting? 56 The sting of death is sin; and the power of sin is the law: 57 but thanks be to God, who giveth us the victory through our Lord Jesus Christ. 58 Wherefore, my beloved brethren, be ye stedfast, unmoveable, always abounding in the work of the Lord, forasmuch as ye know that your labor is not vain in the Lord.

In writing of the resurrection of believers, Paul has been discussing an event which takes place, not at the time of death, but at the return of Christ. One further question, therefore, remains to be answered: What will be the fate of those who are living when Christ returns? Must they die, in order to share the blessedness of those who are raised from the dead?

Their bodies must surely undergo a change. With this assertion Paul begins the paragraph: "Flesh and blood cannot inherit the kingdom of God," that is to say, the human body, the substance of which is flesh and the life-giving principle of which is blood, is not adapted to the future state; it is not fitted for the heavenly world. Then Paul adds, "Neither doth corruption inherit incorruption"; a dead body surely is not to be the dwelling place of an immortal soul. Thus, to be ready for future glory, there must be a change of the body, whether of the living or the dead.

As to this change of the living, Paul declares that he has a revelation, "Behold, I tell you a mystery." Now, a mystery in the language of the apostle is not something concealed, but something once concealed and now revealed. "We all shall not sleep." Not all Christians are to die. Some will be living when Christ comes. Their bodies will be transformed.

The change will be as instantaneous as the moving of an eyelid. It will be announced by "the last trump." Of course Paul does not refer to a literal trumpet, nor to the trumpets of the Apocalypse; nor can one imagine the nature of this divine signal. In the First Epistle of Paul to the Thessalonians it is associated with "the voice of the archangel": "For the Lord himself shall descend from heaven, with a shout, with the voice of the archangel, and with the trump of God: and the dead in Christ shall rise first; then we that are alive, that are left, shall together with them be caught up in the clouds, to meet the Lord in the air."

Again the apostle affirms the necessity of this transformation of living and dead, and then declares that it will be the fulfillment of the Scriptural prophecy of the ultimate triumphant delivery of the people of God; "for this corruptible [the body that is dead] must put on incorruption, and this mortal [the body that is living] must put on immortality."

"Then shall come to pass the saying that is written, Death is swallowed up in victory." Then, but not now, can we speak of real victory. For a time death does triumph. It is useless to deceive ourselves. Death is a reality, death is an enemy, death does conquer and destroy; but his conquest is only for a time. When Christ comes, when the dead are raised and the living are transformed, then in all reality death will be swallowed up in victory.

"The sting of death is sin"; it is sin which imparts bitterness to death, which gives it its penal character, its poignancy, its disgrace. "The power of sin is the law"; for it is the law which gives to sin its power. Human experience has ever found that the demands of the law and its threats only exasperate and drive the soul into more grievous fault. Through Christ, God delivers the believer from both these hostile powers. He removes the sense of guilt and the dread of judgment; and by his Spirit he gives the power to fulfill all that the law demands. Yes, this deliverance is now granted; but when we are set free from all the burdens and losses and sorrows which death has brought, when we know the real liberty of the sons of God, and find righteousness our continual joy as we dwell in our Father's heavenly home, then with truer gladness we will take up the cry, "Thanks be to God, who giveth us the victory."

Having placed before his readers such a vision of the ineffable glory awaiting them, as this chapter reveals, Paul closes his great discussion with the practical exhortation: "Wherefore, . . . be ye stedfast, unmovable, always abounding in the work of the Lord, forasmuch as ye know that your labor is not in vain in the Lord."

III
CONCLUSION
Ch. 16

A. THE COLLECTION FOR THE POOR
AT JERUSALEM   Ch. 16:1-4

1 Now concerning the collection for the saints, as I gave order to the churches of Galatia, so also do ye.   2 Upon the first day of the week let each one of you lay by him in store, as he may prosper, that no collections be made when I come.   3 And when I arrive, whomsoever ye shall approve, them will I send with letters to carry your bounty unto Jerusalem: 4 and if it be meet for me to go also, they shall go with me.

It is a matter of very little moment whether the instruction concerning the offering for the Christian poor at Jerusalem is regarded as the eleventh and last specific topic of this epistle, or whether it is treated as the first paragraph of a concluding chapter.

To the mind of the apostle, at least, this collection was of the very greatest importance; and it is not difficult to interpret his deep concern.

First of all, he would be moved by Christian sympathy to seek for the relief of his fellow believers, particularly when they were his own countrymen.   Then, too, at the Council in Jerusalem, when accepting the commission to the Gentile world he had promised to remember these poor saints.   His chief motive, however, was the desire to knit together the two elements of the church, the Gentile and Jewish, by such an act of charity as would express to the latter both the sympathy of the Gentile Christians and the genuineness of their faith.

Why there were so many poor among the Christians in

Jerusalem is likewise easy to understand. This was not due solely, as is sometimes maintained, to the mistaken experiment of Christian communism. This practice of the community of goods had been only temporary, occasional, and voluntary. The more probable and permanent cause was the persecution and social ostracism suffered by Christians in Jerusalem at the hands of their fellow citizens.

In a city of which the prosperity depended in large measure upon Jewish rites and ceremonies, converts to Christianity would have peculiar difficulty in securing employment and obtaining financial support.

In any case, the needs of these Christians were very great, and for their relief Paul endeavored to secure contributions from all the churches he had founded.

The matter had been proposed to the Corinthians, but little had been done. Therefore Paul here repeats the instructions he had given to the churches of Galatia. These instructions are of the very greatest value to the churches of today. Together with the other intimations of this paragraph, they embody most of the necessary principles of Christian beneficence and church finance.

1. Offerings should be made by every member of the congregation. "Let each one of you lay by him in store." Rich and poor, old and young, all should have a part in church contributions.

2. These offerings should be systematic. They should be made by everyone, every week. "The first day of the week" was already recognized in the time of Paul as the Lord's Day, the resurrection day. It is a good time for such a regular act of Christian worship, as a contribution to support the work of the Lord.

3. A third principle is that of proportionate giving. Some can give more and some less. Each should give "as he may prosper." A definite fraction of the income, as, for example, a tithe, gives system to one's benevolent offerings. The amounts given aggregate more and the burden is less than when gifts are made spasmodically and irregularly.

4. Dependence is not to be placed upon occasional emotional appeals. Thus Paul expresses his desire "that no collections be made when I come." He wished to devote himself to the instruction of the Corinthians, and not to occupy his time with this matter of the collection when he reached Corinth. His visit would have offered a great occasion for a large offering, but he wished this matter to be disposed of before his arrival.

5. Appeals should be made to the highest motives. Not unnaturally do many readers desire to unite this paragraph, relating to the offering, with the chapter which precedes, as an integral part of the epistle. After dwelling on the glory of the resurrection victory and of the future life, Paul adds with surprising abruptness: "Now concerning the collection for the saints." The resurrection was a reason for the offering. This collection was part of "the work of the Lord" in which believers were to abound in view of the victory which was theirs "through our Lord Jesus Christ."

6. Benevolent funds must be carefully administered. The Corinthians are to appoint a financial committee, a board of trustees, to care for the contributions. To these men, who are to be carefully selected, Paul, on his arrival, will give letters of commendation to the church at Jerusalem. There is something pathetic in this provision. Paul's motives had been questioned. Odious insinuations had been made as to his personal interest in these benevolent gifts. He will now guard against giving the least ground for suspicion. Such provision, however, should always be made for the administering of benevolent funds. Business methods must be adopted, and every occasion for suspicion be removed.

7. Benevolent offerings should be so generous as to be worthy of Christ and his servants. Paul intimates that he may go to Jerusalem with the gifts of the churches, if these gifts are large enough to give dignity to such a journey. If it proves to "be meet" for him to go, the messengers from the church may accompany him.

Some offerings are contemptible not because they are so small, but because they are so far less than they might be. They put to shame the church and its representatives. Men feel disgraced to report such inadequate amounts. The gifts of Christians should be in keeping with the claims of those who profess to sit loosely by the things of earth and to be heirs of the heavenly Kingdom of Christ.

B. THE VISITS OF PAUL, TIMOTHY, AND APOLLOS   Ch. 16:5-12

5 But I will come unto you, when I shall have passed through Macedonia; for I pass through Macedonia; 6 but with you it may be that I shall abide, or even winter, that ye may set me forward on my journey withersoever I go. 7 For I do not wish to see you now by the way; for I hope to tarry a while with you, if the Lord permit. 8 But I will tarry at Ephesus until Pentecost; 9 for a great door and effectual is opened unto me, and there are many adversaries.

10 Now if Timothy come, see that he be with you without fear; for he worketh the work of the Lord, as I also do: 11 let no man therefore despise him. But set him forward on his journey in peace, that he may come unto me: for I expect him with the brethren. 12 But as touching Apollos the brother, I besought him much to come unto you with the brethren: and it was not at all his will to come now; but he will come when he shall have opportunity.

In treating of the offering for the poor, Paul has referred to his approaching visit at Corinth. He now deals more at length with his plans. Instead of leaving Ephesus at an early date and sailing directly westward to Corinth, he finds it necessary to prolong his stay in Ephesus and he now purposes to come to Corinth by way of Macedonia. He emphasizes the fact that he will "pass through Macedonia," either to indicate a change of plan, or, as some suppose, to show that his journey is to be of the nature of

an evangelistic tour, on which he will complete the work
begun on his former mission.

There is another reason for delay. If he came at once,
he might have to deal severely with the members of the
Corinthian church. He wishes to give them time in which
to adjust some of the painful matters to which he has
referred.

The cause for delay upon which he dwells, however, is
the fact that there is at Ephesus such an opportunity for
service, "a great door and effectual is opened unto me."
Furthermore, "there are many adversaries," which is another reason for delay, for he must combat them in the
interests of the work.

While his coming to Corinth is being thus delayed, his
visit, when he arrives, will be the more prolonged. He
does not desire merely to pass through the city, but to
remain there for some time. The affairs of the church
demand careful and unhurried action. He may even spend
the winter there, and give them an opportunity of setting
him forward on his journey, either to Jerusalem, as the
case proved, or westward to Rome toward which his heart
was turning.

Timothy had been sent to Corinth. The time, even the
event, of his arrival is uncertain. If he does come, the
apostle bespeaks for him a cordial reception. His youth,
his natural timidity, his sensitiveness, possibly his lack of
culture, might induce the Corinthians to treat him with
disrespect. Paul reminds them that Timothy is engaged
in the service of Christ, as truly as Paul is himself, and so
is worthy of the most considerate treatment. His mission
was delicate and difficult, but the apostle urges them to
send Timothy back to him in peace.

Paul would gladly have sent a more mature messenger,
even Apollos. He had, indeed, urged him to go. However, Apollos was very emphatic in his refusal. It would
seem that he was highly displeased with the party dissen-
sions at Corinth which made it appear that he was a rival

of Paul. Of all such rivalry he was innocent, and he insisted upon delaying his visit until conditions in the Corinthian church were more favorable. Meanwhile Timothy had been sent, and with deep solicitude Paul was awaiting the report which he and his companions might bring.

C. FINAL EXHORTATIONS AND GREETINGS
Ch. 16:13-24

13 Watch ye, stand fast in the faith, quit you like men, be strong. 14 Let all that ye do be done in love.

15 Now I beseech you, brethren (ye know the house of Stephanas, that it is the firstfruits of Achaia, and that they have set themselves to minister unto the saints), 16 that ye also be in subjection unto such, and to every one that helpeth in the work and laboreth. 17 And I rejoice at the coming of Stephanas and Fortunatus and Achaicus: for that which was lacking on your part they supplied. 18 For they refreshed my spirit and yours: acknowledge ye therefore them that are such.

19 The churches of Asia salute you. Aquila and Prisca salute you much in the Lord, with the church that is in their house. 20 All the brethren salute you. Salute one another with a holy kiss.

21 The salutation of me Paul with mine own hand. 22 If any man loveth not the Lord, let him be anathema. Marana tha. 23 The grace of the Lord Jesus Christ be with you. 24 My love be with you all in Christ Jesus. Amen.

As Paul brings his epistle to a close, his exhortations ring out with all the clearness and conciseness of military commands: watch, stand fast, be brave, be strong, be kind.

He expresses the keen delight and refreshment which he has found in the presence and messages of the delegates from Corinth. In particular he mentions Stephanas, who, with his household, was the first Greek convert to Christ, and who had devoted himself to the service of the church. Such men, Paul insists, are worthy of all deference, and their leadership one may safely follow.

Of the final greetings, the first is from the churches of Asia, not only of Ephesus but of the whole province. Paul had not visited all these Christian communities; but he was surrounded by their representatives, he knew their sympathy for the Corinthians, and he loved to bind the churches together by these expressions of love.

The second is from Paul's personal friends, Aquila and Prisca, who might be remembered as Paul's hosts while he was in Corinth, and who subsequently had risked their lives for his sake. With their salutation is united that of their family and of all the Ephesian Christians who met in their hospitable home for worship.

In fact, in the next salutation the whole Christian brotherhood at Ephesus is included: "All the brethren salute you."

In response to these expressions of spiritual affection, the readers were enjoined to express their fellowship in Christ by the ceremonial greeting, the "holy kiss."

Now Paul solemnly places upon the manuscript his sign manual, his autographed salutation. It consists of (1) the title of the greeting: "The salutation of me Paul with mine own hand."

Then follows (2) a double motto. The first clause pronounces accursed, "anathema," anyone who professes faith in Christ and yet feels no real affection for the Lord. The second clause consists of two Aramaic words, "Marana tha," often understood to mean "O Lord, come"; which recalls the prayer closing the Apocalypse, "Come, Lord Jesus." Others find in the words the prophetic promise, "The Lord is coming," "his return is near," "the Lord is at hand," "Marana tha."

Having uttered this great watchword of the waiting church, Paul adds (3) his personal benediction. It is in his favorite words of farewell: "The grace of the Lord Jesus Christ be with you." Here, however, as in no other epistle, he closes with further words of tenderness and love. He has been compelled to rebuke his readers severely; he has heard of their divisions, but now he assures them all of his affection: "My love be with you all in Christ Jesus. Amen."